The
Eat Raw
KITCHEN

The Eat Raw KITCHEN

*Feel-good food for
happy and healthy eating*

This edition published by Parragon Books Ltd in 2016
and distributed by

Parragon Inc.
440 Park Avenue South, 13th Floor
New York, NY 10016
www.parragon.com/lovefood

LOVE FOOD is an imprint of Parragon Books Ltd

ISBN 978-1-4748-3802-3

Printed in China

New recipes and introduction by Judith Wills
Cover photography by Tony Briscoe
New recipe photography by Al Richardson and
home economy and food styling by Laurie Perry

NOTES FOR THE READER

This book uses standard kitchen measuring spoons and cups.
All spoon and cup measurements are level unless otherwise
indicated. Unless otherwise stated, milk is assumed to be
whole, eggs are large, individual fruits and vegetables are
medium, pepper is freshly ground black pepper, and salt is
table salt. A pinch of salt is calculated as $1/16$ teaspoon. Unless
otherwise stated, all root vegetables should be peeled prior
to using.

The times given are an approximate guide only. Preparation
times will differ according to the techniques used by
different people.

Any recipes using sprouting seeds, sometimes called salad
sprouts, should be avoided by children younger than five,
older adults, pregnant women, and those with weakened
immune systems, who are particularly vulnerable to the
bacteria that may be present on sprouts.

Please note that any ingredients stated as being optional are
not included in the nutritional values provided. The nutritional
values given are approximate and provided as only a
guideline; they do not account for individual cooks, measuring
skills, and portion sizes. The nutritional values provided are
per serving or per item.

CONTENTS

WHY RAW FOOD?

As more people around the world realize that true health comes from choosing a natural lifestyle and diet, there has been a significant increase in the number of people looking for a perfect healthy, clean, and environmentally sound way to eat. For hundreds of thousands of these people, a diet that meets these requirements can be summed up by two words: eating raw.

Eating raw food can best be described as a philosophy or a number of choices that don't follow a set of rules. There is some disagreement on what constitutes raw food, but most raw food eaters will agree that the diet consists of fresh, wholesome food that has not been cooked above a temperature of 104°F, has not been highly processed, has not had important elements removed, and has not been adulterated with unnatural additives.

Such a diet usually consists of vegetables, fruits, seeds, nuts, sprouts, and plant oils. While some people following a raw food diet will also eat raw meat, fish, dairy produce, and eggs, the recipes in this book are based on plant foods alone and are, therefore, suitable for a vegan diet.

WHO MAY BENEFIT FROM EATING RAW?

There are many potential health benefits in eating a raw food diet. Raw foodists, as they are sometimes termed, frequently say they have noticed several of the following advantages after just a few weeks of raw eating: improved digestion; improved immunity to health problems, such as colds and eczema; reduction in fluid retention and bloating; an end to food cravings; increased mental and physical energy; better skin; and an improved mood.

The raw food diet is believed to help reverse type-2 diabetes or prevent the condition from getting worse. It is also a natural and simple way to lose weight, and in the long term it may offer protection against the diseases of aging, such as cardiovascular disease, cancers, and arthritis. This may be because of the high levels of antioxidant plant compounds in the diet, the preservation of nutrients that would otherwise be destroyed by cooking, and the avoidance of so-called junk foods.

Eating raw can also help conserve our world by reducing the amount of energy we consume, and it is perhaps the ideal way to eat for those concerned with food sustainability and environmental impact. Many raw food eaters also prefer to choose organic and in-season foods.

YOUR CHOICE

Whether you choose to eat 50 percent, 75 percent, or 100 percent raw, including healthy raw foods and meals more often in your diet is a positive choice and one you will not regret.

SO WHAT IS A RAW FOOD DIET?

The raw vegan diet is typically made up of 75 percent fruits and vegetables in addition to seaweed, sprouted seeds, grains, and legumes, dried fruits, and nuts. The recipes that follow demonstrate just how versatile this selection of foods can be.

RAW FOOD STAPLES
- Fruits, such as oranges, bananas, raspberries, blueberries, and avocado
- Fresh vegetables, such as carrots, parsnips, beans, and cucumber
- Leafy greens, including kale, spinach, broccoli, cabbage, and lettuce
- Soaked raw nuts and seeds
- Sprouted grains, such as quinoa, millet, and buckwheat
- Sprouted legumes, including lentils, chickpeas, and beans
- Probiotic-rich foods, such as raw yogurt and raw sauerkraut

FOODS TO LOOK FOR
Frozen fruit and vegetables are raw as long as they haven't been steamed or boiled to blanch before freezing, so it's best to avoid packaged frozen fruit and vegetables.

Canned foods, such as beans or vegetables, are not raw, because the canning process uses high heat.

Pasteurized foods are not raw due to the process involved. In the United States, this includes most almonds, which are pasteurized by law. Exceptions include raw almonds sold direct to the public by almond growers and imported raw almonds.

Some dried herbs and spices, such as black pepper, cloves, cumin, and nutmeg, are considered raw.

Condiments, such as soy sauce and most others sold in a bottle or jar, are not raw, but some raw foodists eat them in moderation. Alternatives are nama shoyu, an unpasteurized soy sauce (technically, it is heated) or raw coconut aminos, made from coconut sap and aged naturally.

Sugars can be substituted. A good raw option is Medjool dates, which can be soaked and pureed, raw agave nectars, stevia, and coconut palm sugar. Maple syrup is also used—not raw, but some brands are less processed than others. Raw honey is fine (although not vegan) and can be used in place of agave nectar or maple syrup.

Raw salts include sun-dried sea salt and Himalayan pink salt. Standard table salt is not raw.

WHAT CAN I DRINK?
Many who follow a raw food diet like to avoid the impurities present in tap water and even filtered water; they prefer alkalized water or ionized water. Use what you feel comfortable with.

Smoothies and juices made from raw ingredients are fine and nutritious.

Tea and coffee are often avoided because the leaves/beans are processed using heat. Home-picked herbal teas are an excellent alternative.

Alcohol is avoided, but wine is considered a raw item. Organic wines contain fewer sulfites.

Any increase in the amount of raw food you eat will probably be good for your health. If you want to adopt a strict raw diet, it is wise to make a gradual transition to raw food. So if you are vegan, for example, you could increase the amount of raw food you eat by a little each week.

Similarly, if you are currently following a standard diet incorporating cooked meat, fish, and eggs, start the transition to raw food slowly, gradually increasing your intake of vegetables, fruit, and nuts by replacing animal products. If, during this time, you have any discomfort in your digestive tract or bowels, take things more slowly.

You can also choose a long-term high raw diet but still include some non-raw items, either as a vegan, vegetarian, or still eating a little fish, dairy, or meat. Many choose to do this, and any increase in raw food will probably have associated benefits.

The above ideas will help you avoid any "detox" symptoms, such as headache or stomach upset, which can occur if you change your diet too quickly, as well as minimizing the chance of getting cravings for sweet, salty, or junk foods. Any cravings should disappear within two weeks.

Some raw ingredients, such as unsweetened creamed coconut, are available at health-food stores or online. Raw milk is available in some U.S. states directly from a farm, and you can make your own raw milk yogurt using a starter culture available online, but be aware that raw milk and products made from raw milk, such as yogurt and cheese, carry dangerous, even fatal, health risks, especially for children, pregnant women, people with a weakened immune system, and the elderly. Raw coconut yogurt is used throughout this book.

GETTING ENOUGH NUTRIENTS

A typical well-balanced, raw food vegan diet will contain most of the vitamins, minerals, and other nutrients that you need for good health. To help make sure you get a good balance:

* Eat plenty to provide your body with enough calories. Raw vegan eating is an excellent way to lose weight because many plant foods provide bulk for few calories—they have a high water content. However, you need to eat enough to give your body the energy and nutrients it needs. so Include plenty high-calorie items, such as nuts, seeds, fruits naturally high in sugar (such as dates and bananas), and root vegetables, to provide the calories you need daily (around 2,500 for adult males and 2,000 for females, depending on your age). If you are active, you may need more.

* Eat a wide range of foods. The raw vegan diet avoids all animal products, so it is important to get a wide range of other foods every day.

An easy way to get a good variety of vitamins, plant chemicals, and minerals is to have several different colors on your plate at each meal (for example, dark green, orange, red, and purple), while a range of types of food (for example, leaves, fruits, seeds, nuts, and legumes) should ensure you get enough of the amino acids that make up complete protein, as well as adequate carbohydrate, fat, and minerals.

RAW FOOD EQUIPMENT

Because raw food is not cooked, the emphasis is always on the preparation of ingredients. While there are some pieces of equipment that will make your life easier, if you plan to focus on a raw food diet, all you need is a selection of sharp knives and an electric blender.

A range of good knives should include an 8-inch sharp chef's knife for chopping vegetables and fruit; a serrated knife with a blunt end with a 5-inch blade for slicing; and a similar small straight-edge knife for peeling vegetables and fruit. An electric blender is indispensable for making smoothies, blended soups, and purees. A processor will also make light work of chopping, grinding, and making nut butters.

Useful, but not essential, is a dehydrator, a small electric "oven" with racks and trays inside for drying foods, such as crackers and fruits, without cooking them. It improves the texture and variety of the food you prepare. Dehydrators come with several heat settings. The recipes in this book use high (140°F) and low (115°F), but your appliance may have different settings—check the manufacturer's instructions. Some raw food dieters use only the lower settings—they don't consider anything over 118°F as being raw.

If you don't want to buy a dehydrator, your electric oven may have a setting low enough to dehydrate foods at the right heat. It may be the defrost setting or a designated dehydrate setting. To check the temperature of your oven on a setting, use an oven thermometer. A standard oven, unless it has a dehydrate setting, won't be able to dehydrate in the same way as a dehydrator, so using an oven may mean that what you are preparing may not be 100-percent raw.

A juicer is invaluable for juicing fruits and vegetables, a method that removes the insoluble fiber, allowing you to better absorb the nutrients in the fruit and vegetables. The best juicer for preserving the nutrients is a masticating (slow) juicer. Smoothies are also a popular choice—these retain all the goodness and fiber of the contents, but slow down digestion and therefore keep you full for longer. Because oxidization occurs with blending, which undermines the nutritional value of the contents, shorter blending times are advisable. It's best to do the bulk of your blending on a low speed, which doesn't create much oxidation, and limit the amount of time blending on a high speed.

Handheld and freestanding mandoline slicers are useful for slicing fruit and vegetables quickly and efficiently. Interchangeable blades mean you can also dice, make "fries," and so on. A spiralizer can be used for making "spaghetti" using vegetables, such as zucchini and squash.

It is important to practice good kitchen hygiene to avoid contact with harmful bacteria and molds—so wash your hands before preparing foods, eat foods as fresh as you can, and store them in cool conditions. If you share a kitchen with people who eat animal produce, keep separate cutting boards and utensils for yourself to avoid contamination.

RAW FOOD PREPARATION

NUT SOAKING

Many raw eaters prefer to soak nuts to make them more easily digested, activate the beneficial enzymes, and increase the availability of the nutrients. Soaked nuts can also be processed more quickly to make butters and dips. Nuts are usually soaked for 8–12 hours. After soaking and draining, you can dehydrate them (12 hours or more will be necessary) and store as for unsoaked nuts.

NUT BUTTERS

Recipes in this book requiring nut butters include methods for making them in the recipe, but store-bought raw versions are available at health-food stores—make sure the label states they are raw and sugar-free.

SPROUTING

You can sprout your own seeds, legumes, grains, and nuts by using the jar or the tray method. In each case, soak the seeds overnight in water, then drain. Wash sprouts well before eating and consume them soon after harvesting.

For the jar method, add seeds to a sealed jar with 1–2 tablespoons water and cover the top of the jar with cheesecloth before putting an outer lid over the cloth. Invert the jar over a tray, slightly tilted (propped against the wall of the tray) so air can get into the jar. Let stand at room temperature and drain and rinse twice a day until the seeds sprout.

For the tray method, you can buy a variety of single or multitiered sprouting trays or simply use a seed-growing flat tray lined with strong paper towels. Keep the paper wet and rinse and drain the seeds twice a day until they sprout.

RAW COCONUT YOGURT

Raw coconut yogurt is a great addition to the raw food diet. You can also buy raw coconut yogurt already prepared. Coconut yogurt is featured in a number of the recipes in this book. This method will produce a medium-thick yogurt, but you can adjust the amount of coconut water to make yogurt of a thickness to your own preference. This makes around $2\frac{1}{2}$ cups or 4 servings.

Ingredients

$\frac{2}{3}$ cup raw coconut water
1 coconut, white meat only (about ten 2-inch squares), or 2 cups frozen raw white coconut meat (about 1 pound), thawed if frozen, coarsely chopped
2 probiotic powder capsules, found in health-food stores or online

Method

1. Process the coconut meat with a little of the coconut water until it is thoroughly blended, then add the rest of the water and blend again until smooth.

2. Break open the probiotic capsules and sprinkle the powder contents into the blender; pulse for a few seconds.

3. Pour the mixture into a large, wide-neck jar. Put the lid on and let the jar stand in a warm kitchen or room for up to 16 hours, until you have a yogurt mixture. Flavor as you prefer. You can store the yogurt in the refrigerator for several days.

F.A.Q. ABOUT RAW FOOD

WHY ARE UNCOOKED FOODS BEST?

Raw food eaters believe that cooking food destroys much of its nutrients, including vitamins, minerals, enzymes, and plant chemicals. They also believe that raw food is more easily digested and absorbed by the body.

WILL I GET ENOUGH NUTRIENTS?

People on a vegan raw food diet can struggle to get enough calcium, iron, and vitamin B12. The best raw sources of calcium include nuts, seeds, and leafy greens. Good sources of iron in a raw diet include legumes, nori seaweed, nuts and seeds, dark leafy greens, and dried apricots. Vitamin B12 is not usable by humans from a nonanimal source, so if you are not consuming foods fortified with a supplement, you will need to take vitamin B12 supplements. These are readily available. Take one daily if it provides 10 micrograms (mcg) or once a week if it provides 2,000 mcg.

A raw food diet that includes animal and/or dairy produce is unlikely to provide any deficiencies.

WHERE WILL I GET MY PROTEIN?

Legumes, such as lentils and chickpeas, as well as hemp seeds and quinoa, are good sources of protein and all can be eaten raw when sprouted. Fresh legumes, such as peas and edamame (soybeans) are useful sources, while a wide range of vegetables contain protein in differing amounts. As long as you get a variety and sufficiency of protein-containing foods every day, you will not be lacking in any necessary amino acids. Raw milk yogurt is also a good source.

WILL I NEED TO TAKE SUPPLEMENTS?

If you have an adequate and varied diet, there should be no need to take supplements, with the exception of vitamin B12 (see column to left).

WILL PREPARING FOOD TAKE AGES?

You can spend as little or as much time on food preparation as you want. Raw salads, smoothies, and soups are quick to prepare. Some dishes require more chopping, processing, and preparation but a processor and blender, and perhaps a mandoline slicer, save time. Cooking time is zilch—and if you use a dehydrator, it needs little tending while food is dried. "Plan ahead" is the best tip.

SHOULD I USE ORGANIC FRUITS AND VEGETABLES?

Many raw food eaters prefer to eat organically so they know they are eating only natural, unprocessed foods. The flavor and nutrient content of raw plant foods may be superior to nonorganic.

WILL I EXPERIENCE PHYSICAL SYMPTOMS?

Introduce yourself to raw eating gradually and you should not experience adverse symptoms. Your bowels may become more regular due to the additional fiber and water in your diet. Initially, you may get a headache, especially if you are withdrawing from caffeine-rich drinks. Most people report a range of positive improvements in how they feel a few weeks into their raw diet, including having more energy, improvements in digestion, better skin, and better sleep.

BREAKFASTS

Blueberry and oats pie 20

Acai and berry morning jar 22

Buckwheat breakfast bowl 24

Pear, banana, and apple breakfast bowl 26

Very berry overnight oats 28

Buckwheat granola bars 30

Natural blackberry bars 32

Wake-up salad 34

Beet and pomegranate smoothie bowl 36

Morning power bowl smoothie 38

Matcha power smoothie 40

Power gulp 42

BLUEBERRY AND OATS PIE

Here's a delicious, fiber-rich, oat-filled dish packed with fruit, served with a sweet, sticky, and crunchy crumb topping. Everyone will love it.

SERVES: 2
PREP: 15 MINS, PLUS SOAKING

1 cup raw rolled oats
1½ teaspoons chia seeds
2½ tablespoons raw dried coconut flakes
¾ teaspoon ground cinnamon
1 banana, peeled and coarsely chopped
juice of ¼ lemon
1¾ tablespoons raw honey
½ cup blueberries
1 cup raw coconut milk
2 tablespoons chopped raw almonds
½ tablespoons milled flaxseed
1 tablespoon sunflower seeds

1. Combine the oats, chia seeds, 2 tablespoons of the coconut flakes, and ½ teaspoon of the cinnamon in a mixing bowl.

2. Put the banana pieces into a small bowl. Sprinkle with the lemon juice and stir in 1 tablespoon of the honey, making sure each piece of banana is coated with the mixture. (You can warm the honey slightly if it's too solid to stir in.)

3. Stir the bananas, half the blueberries, and the coconut milk into the oat mixture and combine. Spoon evenly into two serving bowls, pressing the banana pieces into the oats. Cover the bowls with plastic wrap or aluminum foil and refrigerate overnight.

4. Meanwhile, start making the pie topping. In a small bowl, stir the almonds, flaxseed, and sunflower seeds together. Stir in the remaining cinnamon and honey, warmed, if necessary. Mix thoroughly and let stand, covered, for the morning.

5. Before serving, sprinkle the topping over the oats and decorate with the remaining coconut flakes and blueberries.

WARM OATS
While oats taste great served cold, they can also be warmed gently to 104°F before you add the topping.

PER SERVING: 582 CALS | 29.6G FAT | 17.1G SAT FAT | 75G CARBS | 29.4G SUGARS | 14.6G FIBER | 12G PROTEIN | TRACE SODIUM

ACAI AND BERRY MORNING JAR

This breakfast jar is pretty to look at and quick to make.
After chilling it in the refrigerator overnight, all you need to do is add
the topping for breakfast—or, indeed, any meal of the day.

SERVES: 1
PREP: 10 MINS, PLUS RESTING AND CHILLING

2/3 cup strawberries
3/4 cup raspberries
1/4 cup blueberries
2/3 cup raw coconut yogurt (see recipe below)
1/4 cup raw coconut milk
1/2 teaspoon seeds from 1 vanilla bean
1 tablespoon chia seeds
2 teaspoons raw honey
1 teaspoon acai powder
1/2 tablespoons lemon juice
2 tablespoons raw cashew butter
1 teaspoon hemp seeds
2 fresh mint sprigs

RAW COCONUT YOGURT

1/2 fresh coconut, white meat only (about five 2-inch squares), or 1 cup frozen raw white coconut meat (about 8 ounces), thawed if frozen, coarsely chopped
1/2 cup raw coconut water
1 probiotic powder capsule

1. To make the coconut yogurt, blend the coconut meat and coconut water in a blender until smooth. Empty the powder from the probiotic capsule into the mixture and blend again for a few seconds.

2. Pour the coconut mixture into a bowl, cover with plastic wrap or aluminum foil, and let stand in the kitchen overnight at warm room temperature. In the morning, you should have about 1 1/4 cups yogurt. Remove what you need and the rest will keep in the refrigerator for up to a week.

3. Blend 1/2 cup of the strawberries, 2/3 cup of the raspberries, and 3 tablespoons of the blueberries with the yogurt, coconut milk, vanilla seeds, chia seeds, honey, acai powder, and lemon juice until smooth. Pour the mixture into a wide-neck jar with a 10–12-ounce capacity. Cover and chill in the refrigerator overnight.

4. The following morning, top with the cashew butter and the remaining berries, followed by the hemp seeds and mint sprigs.

CHIA CHARM
Chia seeds can be used to thicken smoothies and desserts. They also provide essential vitamins, minerals and omega-3 fats.

PER SERVING: 897 CALS | 67.3G FAT | 42.7G SAT FAT | 72.1G CARBS | 34.6G SUGARS | 26.9G FIBER | 15.4G PROTEIN | 40MG SODIUM

BUCKWHEAT BREAKFAST BOWL

Buckwheat has been eaten since Paleolithic times. It makes a tasty cereal and, being a source of complex carbohydrates, provides an excellent boost of energy.

SERVES: 4
PREP: 20–25 MINS, PLUS 36 HRS SPROUTING

1 cup buckwheat
2 cups cold water, preferably filtered
1½ cups raw coconut yogurt
grated zest and juice of 1 orange
3 tablespoons goji berries
¾ cup raspberries
1 Granny Smith apple, cored and diced
1 tablespoon pumpkin seeds
2 passion fruit, pulp only
2 teaspoons ground cinnamon
½ teaspoon ground turmeric
seeds from 1 pomegranate
2 tablespoons agave syrup

1. Rinse the buckwheat three times in fresh water to clean it. Put into a bowl with the cold water and soak for 20 minutes.

2. Drain and rinse the buckwheat, then let stand at room temperature—in either a sprouting tray or a strainer with a bowl beneath—for 36 hours. Rinse the buckwheat if it looks sticky, then again before using.

3. Rinse, drain, and divide the buckwheat among four bowls. Divide the yogurt among the bowls, sprinkle with the remaining ingredients, and serve.

SPROUTING SECRETS
This recipe uses buckwheat that has been sprouted for 36 hours; it can be done in less time, but a longer time provides optimum nutrition.

Note: recipes using buckwheat should be avoided by children younger than five, older adults, pregnant women, and those with weakened immune systems, who are particularly vulnerable to the bacteria that may be present on buckwheat.

PER SERVING: 452 CALS | 22.4G FAT | 17.5G SAT FAT | 58G CARBS | 22.8G SUGARS | 9.8G FIBER | 10.1G PROTEIN | 40MG SODIUM

PEAR, BANANA, AND APPLE BREAKFAST BOWL

If you're tired of eating grains for breakfast, this fruity breakfast bowl will invigorate—it's full of fresh fruity flavors, cinnamon, and delicious dried berries.

SERVES: 2
PREP: 10 MINS, PLUS OPTIONAL CHILLING

2 ripe dessert pears, such as Bartlett
2 green-skinned apples, such as Granny Smith
1 large banana, peeled and chopped
1/3 cup apple juice
juice of 1/2 lemon
2 tablespoons golden raisins
2 tablespoons raw cashew nuts
1 tablespoon sunflower seeds
1 tablespoon raw sugar
1/2 teaspoon ground cinnamon
1 tablespoon goldenberries
1 tablespoon cranberries

1. Core and chop one pear and one apple. Put them into a serving bowl with half the banana and pour over half the apple juice and half the lemon juice. Stir well to combine.

2. Core, peel, and coarsely chop the remaining pear and apple. Add them to a blender with the rest of the banana.

3. Add the remaining apple juice and lemon juice to the blender with the golden raisins and nuts. Blend until you have a finely chopped mixture.

4. Stir the blended mixture into the chopped fruit, along with the sunflower seeds, sugar, and cinnamon. Sprinkle with the goldenberries and cranberries. Chill in the refrigerator, if you have time, or serve immediately.

GOLDEN AND TANGY
Goldenberries are dried ground cherries (aka husk tomatoes)—these small and tangy orange fruits are wrapped in a paper-like husk.

PER SERVING: 438 CALS | 7.5G FAT | 1G SAT FAT | 93.8G CARBS | 62.5G SUGARS | 14.6G FIBER | 5.5G PROTEIN | TRACE SODIUM

VERY BERRY OVERNIGHT OATS

This is a perfect breakfast to bring to work, stored in the jar it is made in. Prepare the oats the night before, and they'll be ready to eat or pick up with no fuss in the morning.

SERVES: 1
PREP: 5 MINS, PLUS SOAKING

½ cup raw rolled oats
1½ teaspoons milled flaxseed
1½ teaspoons acai berry powder
2 teaspoons goji berries
1 tablespoon slivered almonds
1½ teaspoons raw honey
½ cup raw almond milk
2 tablespoons blueberries
3 strawberries

1. Put the oats, flaxseed, acai berry powder, goji berries, most of the slivered almonds, the honey, and almond milk into an 8-ounce jar with a lid. Stir well.

2. Stir a few of the blueberries into the oat mixture. Secure the lid on the jar and chill in the refrigerator overnight.

3. In the morning, chop the strawberries. Top the oats with the remaining blueberries, strawberries, and the remaining almonds.

BERRY ACAI
Acai berry powder is full of fiber, vitamin E, iron, and calcium, and is high in antioxidants.

PER SERVING: 437 CALS | 21.5G FAT | 1.7G SAT FAT | 52.3G CARBS | 15.9G SUGARS | 11.1G FIBER | 13.1G PROTEIN | TRACE SODIUM

BUCKWHEAT GRANOLA BARS

These gorgeous squares are packed with goodness and are simple to make. Because they're rich in protein and healthy fats, they are a great way of keeping hunger at bay throughout the morning.

MAKES: 15 BARS
PREP: 15 MINS, PLUS SOAKING AND COOLING

1 tablespoon melted cold-pressed extra virgin coconut oil, plus 2 teaspoons for brushing
²/₃ cup raw rolled oats
¹/₂ cup ground almonds
¹/₃ cup sunflower seeds
3 tablespoons pumpkin seeds
¹/₃ cup raw pistachio nuts
¹/₂ cup cacao nibs
¹/₄ cup goji berries
¹/₂ oz cup buckwheat groats, soaked in water for 20 minutes, drained, and rinsed
¹/₃ cup chopped dried apricots
2 Medjool dates, pitted and chopped
2 tablespoons raw almond butter
5 tablespoons raw honey

1. Brush a 10 x 6-7-inch dish with coconut oil and line it with enough parchment paper to hang over the sides. Set aside.

2. In a large bowl, combine the oats, ground almonds, seeds, pistachio nuts, cacao nibs, and goji berries, and stir well. Add the soaked buckwheat to the bowl and combine. Stir in the apricots and dates.

3. In a small bowl, combine the almond butter, honey, and coconut oil. Warm on the lowest setting in the microwave for 1 minute, or in a small saucepan over gentle heat, and mix with a fork.

4. Pour the almond butter mixture over the dry ingredients and stir well so that everything is moist.

5. Transfer the granola to the prepared dish and press it down firmly. Cover and refrigerate overnight, or for several hours, then remove from the dish, using the overhanging paper. Peel it off.

6. Cut the granola into 2-inch bars using a sharp knife. Store them in a container with a lid in the refrigerator.

STORAGE
The bars will store in an airtight container in the refrigerator for a week, or they can be frozen.

PER BAR: 180 CALS | 9.6G FAT | 2.4G SAT FAT | 22.9G CARBS | 11.3G SUGARS | 4.2G FIBER | 5.5G PROTEIN | TRACE SODIUM

NATURAL
BLACKBERRY BARS

Two of nature's favorites, blackberries and hazelnuts, meet Caribbean coconut to make creamy bars with a crisp, nutty crust. They are also full of vitamin C and healthy oils.

MAKES: 8 OBLONGS OR 16 SMALL SQUARES
PREP: 20 MINS, PLUS CHILLING

½ cup melted cold-pressed extra virgin coconut oil, plus 1 tablespoon for brushing
1 cup plus 2 tablespoons raw coconut flour
⅓ cup plus 1 ½ tablespoons ground almonds
½ cup chopped raw hazelnuts
⅓ cup chopped raw almonds
1 tablespoon raw sugar
3 tablespoons maple syrup

TOPPING
1¼ cups blackberries
1 cup strawberries
⅔ cup raw coconut flour
juice of 1 lemon
½ cup raw coconut milk
¼ cup raw creamed coconut
¼ cup melted cold-pressed extra virgin coconut oil
¼ cup maple syrup
2 tablespoons cacao nibs

1. Brush an 8-inch baking pan with coconut oil and line it with parchment paper. Set aside.

2. To make the crust, combine the coconut flour, ground almonds, nuts, and sugar in a mixing bowl.

3. Gently warm the coconut oil with the maple syrup on the lowest setting in the microwave for 1 minute, or in a small saucepan over gentle heat. Stir the melted ingredients into the dry ones.

4. Press the mixture into the bottom of the prepared pan. Chill in the refrigerator for an hour, or until the mixture has hardened.

5. Meanwhile, make the topping. Blend the blackberries and strawberries in a blender, then blend in the coconut flour, lemon juice, and coconut milk.

6. Gently warm the creamed coconut with the coconut oil and maple syrup, and combine well. Add to the ingredients in the blender and blend everything for a few seconds.

7. When the crust has chilled, spoon the blackberry mixture evenly over the top. Cover and chill again for about 2 hours. The topping will not be particularly firm but should be firm enough to cut.

8. Grate cacao nibs over the top of the chilled mixture and cut it into 8 oblongs or 16 squares with a sharp knife.

TOP TOPPINGS
For a summertime spin on this recipe, try a mixture of raspberries and strawberries.

PER SMALL SQUARE: 232 CALS | 17G FAT | 11.4G SAT FAT | 17.2G CARBS | 7.4G SUGARS | 6.8G FIBER | 3.8G PROTEIN | TRACE SODIUM

WAKE-UP SALAD

When you want something that isn't sweet for breakfast, try this crunchy salad. It's layered with different fruits and vegetables, and is quick to put together.

SERVES: 2
PREP: 10 MINS

2 cups chopped kale
1 large red-skinned apple, such as Red Delicious, cored and chopped
1 carrot, peeled and thinly sliced
4 Medjool dates, pitted and chopped
2 tablespoons chopped raw walnuts
2 teaspoons sesame seeds
2 teaspoons hemp seeds
2 teaspoons sunflower seeds

DRESSING
3 tablespoons cold-pressed extra virgin canola oil
1 tablespoon raw apple cider vinegar
2 teaspoons stone-ground mustard
2 teaspoons maple syrup
1/2 teaspoon sea salt
1/2 teaspoon black pepper
2 scallions, finely chopped

1. To make the dressing, combine the dressing ingredients in a screw-top jar or small mixing bowl. Shake or stir well.

2. Put the kale into a serving bowl or two individual dishes. Add the apple and carrot, and stir in the dates and walnuts.

3. Pour the dressing over the salad and mix together. Sprinkle with the seeds to serve.

SEED HEALTH
Hemp seeds are a great source of antioxidants. This recipe has unhulled seeds for a richer mineral and fiber content, but you can also use hulled seeds—both are available.

PER SERVING: 555 CALS | 31.9G FAT | 2.5G SAT FAT | 66.2G CARBS | 49.6G SUGARS | 10.1G FIBER | 8.6G PROTEIN | 680MG SODIUM

BEET AND POMEGRANATE SMOOTHIE BOWL

Tender beet and zesty pomegranate seeds creates a fabulous combination. The addition of spinach and wheatgrass makes this tasty breakfast bowl truly healthy.

SERVES: 1
PREP: 10 MINS, PLUS OPTIONAL CHILLING

1 large beet, peeled and chopped
½ cup spinach leaves
3 tablespoons pomegranate seeds
½ cup water
juice of 1 orange
1 tablespoon raw honey
½ cup raw coconut yogurt
1 teaspoon wheatgrass powder
2 teaspoons buckwheat groats
2 round orange slices, halved

1. Put the beet in a blender with the spinach, 2 tablespoons of the pomegranate seeds, and half the water. Blend until smooth.

2. Add the rest of the water, the orange juice, honey, ⅓ cup of the yogurt, and the wheatgrass powder to the blender. Blend again.

3. Pour the smoothie into a serving bowl and chill for an hour or so, if you have time.

4. Drizzle the remaining yogurt over the smoothie. Sprinkle with the groats and decorate with the orange slices and remaining seeds.

FOR A CHANGE OF PACE
Try raspberries instead of pomegranate seeds for a change, or if you want to make this smoothie when pomegranates aren't in season.

PER SERVING: 604 CALS | 32.7G FAT | 28G SAT FAT | 75.7G CARBS | 48.6G SUGARS | 17.6G FIBER | 10.2G PROTEIN | 160MG SODIUM

MORNING POWER BOWL SMOOTHIE

Here's a great way to increase your nutrient intake, with plenty of colorful fruits to provide antioxidants, as well as healthy fats from nuts and seeds.

SERVES: 1
PREP: 10 MINS

¹/₃ cup strawberries
¹/₃ cup blackberries
¹/₃ cup raspberries
1 banana, peeled
²/₃ cup hemp milk
1 tablespoon coconut oil
1 tablespoon ground almonds
1 kiwi, peeled and sliced
2 teaspoons chia seeds
1 small mango, peeled, pitted, and chopped
1 tablespoon chopped walnuts
2 teaspoons toasted sesame seeds

1. Put the strawberries, blackberries, raspberries, half the banana, the hemp milk, coconut oil, and ground almonds into a blender and blend until smooth.

2. Pour into a bowl and place the remaining ingredients on top to serve.

TOP CHOICE
Replace the topping with fruits and nuts of your choice, aiming to use those in season—luscious berries would be great in the summer, sprinkled with freshly shredded mint leaves.

PER SERVING: 654 CALS | 34.4G FAT | 13.8G SAT FAT | 86.9G CARBS | 51.1G SUGARS | 19.5G FIBER | 11.1G PROTEIN | 40MG SODIUM

MATCHA
POWER SMOOTHIE

This is one of the best green smoothies you'll ever try—it's bursting with super ingredients, including spinach and avocado, to jump-start your day.

SERVES: 1
PREP: 5 MINS, PLUS OPTIONAL CHILLING

1 cup spinach
1 banana, peeled and chopped
1 small ripe avocado, peeled, pitted, and coarsely chopped
2 kiwis, peeled and chopped
½ cup raw almond milk
1½ teaspoons raw honey
1 teaspoon matcha tea powder
½ teaspoon wheatgrass powder
2 teaspoons slivered almonds, to decorate
½ teaspoon maca powder, to decorate

1. Blend the spinach, banana, avocado, and one of the kiwis in a blender with half the milk until you have a puree.

2. Add the honey, matcha, wheatgrass, and remaining milk to the blender and blend until smooth. Pour the smoothie into your serving bowl. Chill for an hour, if you have time.

3. Top your smoothie with the remaining kiwi and decorate with the slivered almonds and maca powder.

MAGICAL MATCHA
Matcha is a Japanese green tea rich in catechins, a type of antioxidant that fights cancers and heart disease. When you add matcha powder to a dish, you're getting the full benefit of the leaves instead of simply drinking a brew and discarding the leaves.

PER SERVING: 566 CALS | 30.3G FAT | 3.3G SAT FAT | 72.1G CARBS | 37.4G SUGARS | 18.9G FIBER | 13.2G PROTEIN | 40MG SODIUM

POWER GULP

Beets are a favorite vegetable among sportsmen and sportswomen. They're great for boosting stamina and making muscles work harder, and are packed with vitamins, minerals, carbohydrates, protein, and powerful antioxidants.

SERVES: 4
PREP: 5 MINUTES

2 beets, halved
3 tablespoons flaxseed
4 plums, pitted and quartered
1 cup seedless red grapes
1 cup chilled water ice,
to serve (optional)

1. Feed the beets through a juicer. Put the flaxseed into a blender and blend until finely ground. Add the beet juice, plums, grapes, and water, and blend until smooth. Pour into a glass, add ice, if using, and serve immediately.

BEET POWER
Beets have one of the highest sugar levels of any vegetable, so they give a great energy boost. They also help regulate blood pressure and nerve function.

PER SERVING: 118 CALS | 3.4G FAT | 0.3G SAT FAT | 21.2G CARBS | 15.8G SUGARS | 3.6G FIBER | 2.9G PROTEIN | 40MG SODIUM

LUNCHES AND SNACKS

SPRING ROLLS IN THE RAW

If you've never tried making your own spring rolls, you'll be delighted at how easy they are. These colorful rolls taste delicious and are packed with fiber and antioxidants.

MAKES: 16 HALF-ROLLS, TO SERVE 4
PREP: 15 MINS

8 round rice spring roll wrappers
1 yellow bell pepper, halved, seeded,
and thinly sliced
1 red bell pepper, halved, seeded, and thinly sliced
½ cucumber, halved, seeded and thinly sliced
1 bok choy, leaves separated and stalks sliced
2 carrots, peeled and cut into 4-inch sticks
4 large scallions, sliced lengthwise
2 celery stalks
2 teaspoons raw coconut aminos sauce

COCONUT DIP

1 cup raw coconut yogurt
2 teaspoons raw coconut aminos sauce
½ teaspoon ground cumin seeds
½ teaspoon ground coriander seeds
½ garlic clove, crushed
½ teaspoon sea salt
3 tablespoons chopped fresh cilantro leaves

1. Soak a spring roll wrapper for 10 seconds, or until just pliable, then smooth it on a cutting board. Arrange one-eighth of all the vegetables on the lower center of the wrap. Sprinkle with a little of the coconut aminos sauce.

2. Tuck each side of the wrapper into the center, then fold the lower edge up to enclose the vegetables, keeping them in a tight bunch as you roll up to the top. Repeat with the remaining seven wrappers.

3. Using a sharp knife, cut each roll in half until you have 16 halves and arrange them on a serving dish.

4. To make the dip, combine the yogurt in a mixing bowl with the coconut aminos sauce, cumin, coriander, garlic, salt, and half the cilantro leaves. Spoon the dip into a serving dish and serve alongside the spring rolls, garnished with the remaining cilantro, if desired.

CHANGE THE DIP

For another occasion, try serving the rolls with a nutty dip—just swirl raw cashew butter into some nut milk and add a dash of raw coconut aminos sauce.

PER SERVING: 266 CALS | 13.2G FAT | 11.2G SAT FAT | 35G CARBS | 8.8G SUGARS | 7G FIBER | 4.8G PROTEIN | 640MG SODIUM

CHILLED BEET AND WATERMELON SOUP

Bolstered by sweet flavors and a host of health-giving nutrients, this soup tastes amazing all year round. Serve it chilled for a summer gazpacho, or warmed during the frosty winter months.

SERVES: 4
PREP: 10 MINS, PLUS CHILLING

4 tender beets (about 1¼ pounds), peeled
1 large carrot, peeled
2 cups diced watermelon flesh
juice of ½ lemon
½ cup water
1 teaspoon sea salt
1 teaspoon black pepper
3 tablespoons chopped fresh dill
⅔ cup raw coconut yogurt

1. Blend two-thirds of the beet, carrot, and watermelon in a blender with the lemon juice and most of the water until smooth. Add the salt and pepper, then add the water, a little at a time, and blend again until you have a medium-thick soup texture. Pour the soup into a large bowl.

2. Grate the remaining beet and carrot, and stir into the soup. Stir half of the remaining watermelon into the soup with half the dill.

3. Pour the soup into four serving bowls and drizzle with the yogurt. Sprinkle the remaining watermelon pieces over the top and sprinkle with the rest of the dill. Chill in the refrigerator before serving.

PER SERVING: 209 CALS | 9.9G FAT | 8.4G SAT FAT | 29.6G CARBS | 19G SUGARS | 8.5G FIBER | 4.4G PROTEIN | 760MG SODIUM

GARLIC AND HERB YOGURT DIP

This delicious dip starts with a coconut yogurt recipe that is drained overnight, making a thick Greek-style yogurt. You can flavor it with your own herbs and spices. It is a good source of fiber and healthy probiotics, which are important for digestive health.

SERVES: 4
PREP: 20 MINS, PLUS CHILLING TIME

¼ cup raw coconut water
½ coconut, white meat only (seven to eight 10-inch squares), or 1½ cups frozen raw white coconut meat (about 10½ ounces), thawed if frozen
1 probiotic powder capsule
1 clove garlic
2 tablespoons mixed fresh soft herbs, such as parsley, cilantro, tarragon, or chives
2 tablespoons extra virgin olive oil
2 tablespoons pistachio nuts
14 ounces mixed vegetable sticks, such as asparagus, red bell pepper, cucumber, baby zucchini, babycorn, carrots, and broccoli florets
salt and pepper (optional)

1. Process the coconut meat with half the coconut water in a food processor until it is thoroughly blended, then add the rest of the water and blend again until smooth.

2. Break open the probiotic capsules and sprinkle the powder contents into the food processor; pulse for a few seconds.

3. Pour the mixture into a large, wide-neck jar. Put the lid on and let stand in a warm kitchen or room for up to 16 hours, until you have a yogurt mixture.

4. Spoon the yogurt into a strainer lined with cheesecloth and set over a bowl. Refrigerate for 24 hours or until the yogurt remaining in the strainer is a consistency similar to a soft cheese. Discard any liquid in the bowl.

5. Stir the garlic and herbs into the yogurt and season with salt and pepper, if using.

6. Divide among four bowls, drizzle with the oil, and sprinkle with the chopped nuts. Serve with vegetable sticks for dipping.

PER SERVING: 380 CALS | 34G FAT | 23.5G SAT FAT | 19G CARBS | 8.7G SUGARS | 9.4G FIBER | 4.9G PROTEIN | 40G SODIUM

RAW SAUERKRAUT

Fermented foods, such as sauerkraut and kimchi, are beneficial for the digestive system because they're rich in good bacteria. This sauerkraut recipe is particularly easy and quick to make.

SERVES: 8
PREP: 10 MINS, PLUS FERMENTING

3³/₄ cups shredded red cabbage
1¹/₂ cups shredded green cabbage
2 small carrots, peeled and thinly sliced
1¹/₂-inch piece fresh ginger, peeled
and finely chopped
2¹/₂ teaspoons sea salt

1. Mix all the ingredients together in a large plastic mixing bowl.

2. Firmly knead the mixture for 5 minutes, until the vegetables begin to release their juice and become softer.

3. Pack the mixture into a 24-ounce jar with lid. Press the top of the mixture down and fill up with enough water to completely cover the vegetables.

4. Secure the lid on the jar and keep it at room temperature for a week. Every day, open the jar and press the sauerkraut down again—you should see air bubbles coming out of the top of the mixture. Make sure all the vegetables are completely covered in the liquid.

5. After a week, you can eat the sauerkraut, or store it in a cool place for several weeks.

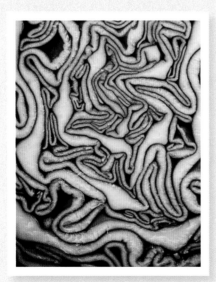

BEET BOOST
Try making a similar recipe using beets instead of carrot. You can also add spices, such as caraway seeds or cumin, to give the sauerkraut a little kick.

PER SERVING: 24 CALS | 0.2G FAT | TRACE SAT FAT | 5.7G CARBS | 2.9G SUGARS | 1.8G FIBER | 1G PROTEIN | 760MG SODIUM

COOL CUCUMBER SUSHI

Who doesn't love a plateful of pretty sushi with tantalizing side dips? These rolls feature homemade cucumber wrappers, a colorful selection of vegetables, and cauliflower rice.

MAKES: 16 SUSHI ROLLS, TO SERVE 4
PREP: 25 MINS

CUCUMBER SKIN SUSHI
1 (12-inch-long) cucumber
3/4 cup cauliflower florets
1 teaspoon cold-pressed extra virgin sesame oil
1 teaspoon raw rice vinegar
1/2 teaspoon salt
1/2 avocado, peeled
2 scallions, finely chopped
1/2 small red bell pepper, finely chopped
sea salt (optional)

SPICY CASHEW DIP
1/2 cup raw cashew nuts, soaked in water
for 1 hour, drained, and rinsed
2 teaspoons finely chopped fresh ginger
2 teaspoons raw wasabi paste

CUCUMBER WRAPPERS
1 (12-inch-long) cucumber
1 3/4 cups baby spinach leaves
1 small zucchini, finely sliced
1 carrot, finely sliced
1/4 cup raw cashew butter

MUSHROOM DRESSING
2 dark-gilled mushrooms, coarsely chopped
1 teaspoon sea salt
1/4 cup water
1 teaspoon finely chopped fresh ginger

1. Cut off the ends of the cucumber so that you have a center section that is one width. Cut into eight pieces, 1 1/2 inches long. Scoop out the seed section and about half the flesh from each piece to form eight hollow sushi rolls. Set aside.

2. Put the cauliflower, sesame oil, rice vinegar, and salt into a food processor and pulse until the mixture resembles cooked rice.

3. Mash the avocado in a small bowl, adding salt, if using.

4. Arrange your cucumber shapes on a board or serving plate and fill each one with some cauliflower rice, pressing it toward the sides. Add some avocado and press it into the rice. Sprinkle with some scallions and red bell pepper.

5. To make the dip, put the soaked nuts into a food processor and process for several minutes, until you have a creamy consistency. Beat in the ginger and wasabi paste, and transfer to a small serving dish.

6. Start making the cucumber wrappers. Trim off the ends of the cucumber as before. Cut the cucumber in half, then cut each half into thin strips lengthwise and discard the first skin layer. You will need 24 strips for the eight rolls.

7. To make each roll, arrange three cucumber strips on a board. Place one-eighth of the spinach leaves at one end in a line from left to right. Arrange one-eighth of the zucchini and carrot slices on top, again in a line from left to right, and one-eighth of the cashew cream.

8. Starting with the filled end, roll up the cucumber strip until you have a filled tube. Transfer the roll to a serving board or plate and continue to make the rest of the sushi.

9. To make the dressing, blend the mushrooms, salt, and water in a clean processor until you have a smooth sauce. Add a little more water to make a soy sauce consistency and stir in the ginger. Serve in a small bowl alongside the sushi.

PER SERVING: 297 CALS | 19.2G FAT | 3.2G SAT FAT | 27.2G CARBS | 9G SUGARS | 5.8G FIBER | 10.1G PROTEIN | 1,000MG SODIUM

JEWEL SALAD WITH RANCH DRESSING

A beautiful salad is always a welcome addition to the dinner table. This vibrant dish is complemented by a protein-rich variation of the traditional ranch dressing.

SERVES: 4
PREP: 20 MINS, PLUS SOAKING

2 large tomatoes, seeded
1 cucumber
½ red onion
1 carrot
1 yellow bell pepper, seeded
10 red radishes
½ cup mixed chopped soft herbs, such as parsley, mint, and cilantro
zest and juice of ½ lemon
¼ cup cold-pressed extra virgin olive oil
½ teaspoon sea salt
½ teaspoon black pepper

RANCH DRESSING
¾ cup raw cashew nuts, soaked in water for 2 hours, drained, and rinsed
1 tablespoon raw apple cider vinegar
½ cup raw coconut milk
1 garlic clove, crushed
½ teaspoon sea salt
2 scallions, finely chopped
2 tablespoons chopped fresh parsley

1. To make the dressing, put the soaked nuts, vinegar, ¼ cup of the coconut milk, the garlic, and salt into a blender. Blend until you have a smooth paste. Add more coconut milk, a little at a time, until you have a fairly thick mix. It should be a cross between a dip and a pouring consistency. Stir in the scallions and parsley.

2. To make the salad, finely chop the vegetables and put them into a large serving bowl or smaller individual ones. Stir in all the remaining salad ingredients and serve.

SYNC WITH THE SEASONS
You can vary the salad ingredients according to what you have, or what is in season. For example, try swapping the yellow bell pepper for corn kernels.

PER SERVING: 360 CALS | 28.8G FAT | 7.2G SAT FAT | 22.7G CARBS | 9.4G SUGARS | 6G FIBER | 7.5G PROTEIN | 600MG SODIUM

CUCUMBER AND BUCKWHEAT YOGURT

Raw yogurt is a wonderful base for all kinds of savory dishes. Make this crunchy and refreshing yogurt jar for an easy lunch or light bite on the go.

SERVES: 4
PREP: 10 MINS, PLUS SOAKING AND CHILLING

1 cucumber, halved, seeded, and chopped
2 cups raw coconut yogurt
3 tablespoons chopped fresh mint
1 teaspoon sea salt
1 teaspoon black pepper
²⁄₃ cup sun-dried raisins
½ cup chopped raw walnuts
¾ cup raw buckwheat groats, soaked in water for
20 minutes, drained, and rinsed
20 fresh mint leaves, to garnish

1. Wrap the cucumber pieces in paper towels and squeeze to release the moisture—the paper towels should end up soaked.

2. Mix the yogurt, mint, salt, and pepper together in a bowl.

3. Divide the ingredients evenly among four 9–10-ounce jars with lids. Layer with the raisins, half the walnuts, the soaked groats, three-quarters of the cucumber, and the yogurt mixture. Garnish with the remaining cucumber and walnuts.

4. Divide the mint leaves among each of the jars and chill for 30 minutes before serving.

INGREDIENT SWAPS
Try finely chopped scallions instead of the mint and add ½ teaspoon of crushed garlic to the yogurt mixture. Fresh, green, new season's garlic is best.

PER SERVING: 659 CALS | 45G FAT | 29.3G SAT FAT | 63.4G CARBS | 23.6G SUGARS | 15.2G FIBER | 12G PROTEIN | 640MG SODIUM

EGGPLANT, LETTUCE, AND AVOCADO SANDWICH

When you want a satisfying raw lunch, you'll fall in love with this sandwich. It's filled with creamy cashew cheese, smashed avocado, and crisp slices of eggplant.

MAKES: 2 SANDWICHES
PREP: 25 MINS, PLUS SOAKING, MARINATING AND DEHYDRATING

CRISPY EGGPLANT
1 large eggplant
2 tablespoons cold-pressed extra virgin olive oil
1 tablespoon raw agave nectar
1 tablespoon raw coconut aminos sauce
2 teaspoons minced fresh mild red chile
1/3 teaspoon sea salt

CASHEW CHEESE
1/2 cup raw cashew nuts, soaked in water for 1 hour, drained, and rinsed
2 garlic cloves
1 tablespoon lemon juice
2 teaspoons raw coconut aminos sauce
1/3 teaspoon sea salt

RED PEPPER PESTO
1 small red bell pepper, coarsely chopped
2 pieces sun-dried tomatoes, soaked in water for 10 minutes, drained, and rinsed
1/4 cup raw pine nuts
1/4 teaspoon sea salt and 1/4 teaspoon black pepper

SMASHED AVOCADO
1 ripe avocado, pitted and peeled
1 scallion, chopped
juice of 1/2 lime and 1/4 teaspoon sea salt
1/4 teaspoon black pepper
1 tablespoon chopped fresh cilantro leaves

4 Boston or small butter lettuce leaves, to serve
1 tomato, sliced, to serve

1. You will need a dehydrator for this recipe. If you don't have a dehydrator, an electric oven may have a setting to dehydrate food on a low enough heat. It may be the defrost setting or slightly higher, or a designated dehydrate setting. Check you have the correct temperature with an oven thermometer before dehydrating in a standard oven.

2. Slice the eggplant into eight long slices, about 1/4 inch thick, and discard the two skin sides. Combine the rest of the ingredients in a small bowl and brush each eggplant slice with the mixture.

3. Put the eggplant in a nonmetallic dish and cover. Let marinate for 2 hours, then drain and layer on a dehydrator tray. (If using the oven, use a nonstick oven pan.) Dehydrate on low (115°F) for 8 hours, turning the slices halfway.

4. Meanwhile, make the cashew cheese. Blend the soaked nuts in a food processor with the remaining ingredients until you have a smooth paste. Thin with a little water, if necessary, and blend again. Remove the cheese from the processor and set aside in a bowl.

5. Make the red pepper pesto. Add the red bell pepper, soaked tomatoes, pine nuts, and salt and pepper to a processor and pulse until you have a thick paste with small visible pieces in it.

6. Before you assemble your sandwiches, make the smashed avocado. In a small bowl, mash the avocado flesh with the rest of the ingredients until you have a textured puree.

7. Prepare your sandwiches on your serving plates. For each sandwich, start with two slices of eggplant side by side. Top with half the cashew cheese and two lettuce leaves. Smooth on half the red pepper pesto and arrange half the tomato slices on top. Add half the avocado mixture and smooth down, then finish with two more eggplant slices. Serve immediately.

PER SERVING: 725 CALS | 51.4G FAT | 7G SAT FAT | 62.5G CARBS | 31.5G SUGARS | 19.2G FIBER | 16.4G PROTEIN | 1,440MG SODIUM

VEGETABLE FRIES WITH CASHEW DIP

Forget about French fries—once you try this mouthwatering raw version with the truly delicious dip, you'll want to make them time and again.

SERVES: 2

PREP: 20 MINS, PLUS SOAKING AND DEHYDRATING

1 small butternut squash
1 zucchini, cut into thin sticks
1 tablespoon cold-pressed extra virgin canola oil
½ teaspoon sea salt
½ teaspoon black pepper

CASHEW DIP

½ cup raw cashew nuts, soaked in water for 2 hours, drained, and rinsed
2 tablespoons raw tahini
1 tablespoon lemon juice
1 garlic clove, crushed
1 carrot, peeled and chopped
¼ teaspoon sea salt
¼ teaspoon black pepper
¼ cup raw almond milk

1. You will need a dehydrator for this recipe. If you don't have a dehydrator, an electric oven may have a setting to dehydrate food on a low enough heat. It may be the defrost setting or slightly higher, or a designated dehydrate setting. Check you have the correct temperature with an oven thermometer before dehydrating in a standard oven.

2. Cut the squash in half between the thin neck and the bulbous bottom. Reserve the bulbous bottom for another dish. Peel the squash and cut it into thin sticks.

3. Toss the zucchini and squash sticks with the canola oil, salt, and pepper, and arrange them on a dehydrator tray. If using the oven, use a nonstick oven pan.) Dehydrate on high (140°F) for an hour, then low (115°F) for 8 hours, turning the sticks halfway.

4. Meanwhile, make the cashew dip. Add the soaked nuts to a blender with the tahini and lemon juice, then process until you have a coarse butter.

5. Add the garlic, carrot, salt, and pepper to the blender and process again until you have a pâté consistency. Remove the mixture and stir in the nut milk, a little at a time, until you have a dip-like consistency—you may not need all the milk, or you may need a little more.

6. When the sticks are crispy and like French fries, remove them from the dehydrator and serve with the dip.

SWEET POTATO FRIES

You can make these fries with sweet potato instead of the squash or zucchini.

PER SERVING: 473 CALS | 33.2G FAT | 4.6G SAT FAT | 39.6G CARBS | 9.8G SUGARS | 8.1G FIBER | 12.9G PROTEIN | 920MG SODIUM

MISO SOUP WITH RADISH AND SEED SPROUTS

Miso soup is a cherished dish eaten in Japan every day. Made from fermented soybeans, miso is the perfect base for a raw soup, because it's rich in protein and beneficial bacteria.

SERVES: 4

PREP: 12 MINS, PLUS SPROUTING

2 tablespoons unshelled sunflower seeds suitable for sprouting

2½ tablespoons organic miso paste

1 large garlic clove

2 teaspoons finely chopped fresh ginger

1½ tablespoons raw rice vinegar

¼ cup water

3 scallions

12 snow peas

4 radishes

8 baby corn

1 cup fresh coconut shards

½ cup pea shoots

1 tablespoon cold-pressed extra virgin sesame oil, to serve

1. Start sprouting the sunflower seeds three days before you want to make the soup. Put them into a shallow dish lined with plenty of thick paper towels. Sprinkle lukewarm water over the seeds and cover with more paper. Sprinkle again. Let stand in a dark, warm place. Check each day that the seeds are still slightly damp. When they begin to sprout, remove the top layer of paper and bring into the light. The sprouts can be eaten when they are about ⅜ inch long.

2. To make the soup, blend the miso paste with the garlic, ginger, rice vinegar, and water in a blender. Add more water until you have 5 cups and stir well. Pour the soup into four bowls.

3. Thinly slice the scallions, snow peas, radishes, and corn, and arrange the vegetables over the soup. Top with the coconut shards, pea shoots, and seed sprouts. Drizzle with the sesame oil to serve.

MISO PASTE

Buy organic, unpasteurized miso paste—some brands are pasteurized, which means the miso is heated above the minimal heat considered acceptable for a raw diet.

Note: recipes using sprouting seeds should be avoided by children younger than five, older adults, pregnant women, and those with weakened immune systems, who are particularly vulnerable to the bacteria that may be present on sprouts.

PER SERVING: 156 CALS | 11.9G FAT | 6.3G SAT FAT | 9.8G CARBS | 3.5G SUGARS | 3.7G FIBER | 3.7G PROTEIN | 40MG SODIUM

VEGETABLE AND SEED CRACKERS

This recipe is ideal for using the leftover pulp from juicing your vegetables—so there's no need to waste all that fiber and goodness. Nibble on one for breakfast or an afternoon snack.

MAKES: 16 CRACKERS
PREP: 10 MINS, PLUS SOAKING AND DEHYDRATING

5 carrots, peeled and coarsely chopped
4 celery stalks, coarsely chopped
1 cup chopped red radishes
2 tablespoons milled flaxseed
1 tablespoon whole golden flaxseed
3 tablespoons sunflower seeds
1 tablespoon pumpkin seeds
1¼ teaspoons sea salt
1½ teaspoons black pepper
1 tablespoon chia seeds, soaked in
3 tablespoons water for 1 hour

1. You will need a dehydrator for this recipe. If you don't have a dehydrator, an electric oven may have a setting to dehydrate food on a low enough heat. It may be the defrost setting or slightly higher, or a designated dehydrate setting. Check you have the correct temperature with an oven thermometer before dehydrating in a standard oven.

2. Juice the carrots, celery stalks, and radishes, and save the juice to drink. Remove the pulp from the juicer and put it into a mixing bowl. You should have about 1½ mugfuls of pulp.

3. Stir the rest of the ingredients into the mixing bowl, including the soaked seeds and their water. Combine thoroughly, adding a little water if the mix seems dry or doesn't stick together well.

4. Spread the mixture thinly and evenly on a dehydrator tray lined with a nonstick sheet. (If using the oven, use a nonstick oven pan.) Dehydrate on low (115°F) for 4 hours. Turn the mixture over, score it into 16 crackers, and dehydrate on low for an additional 4 hours, or until the crackers are crisped to your preference.

5. Let the crackers cool, then break along the knife scores. Store the crackers in an airtight container.

JUICING PROCESS

If you don't have a juicer, you can make the vegetable pulp by pulsing the vegetables in a processor, then simply squeezing the juice from the mix with clean hands. Alternatively, put the mixture in a strainer over a bowl and mash firmly with a pestle or the round end of a rolling pin until the pulp is dry.

PER CRACKER: 29 CALS | 2.1G FAT | 0.2G SAT FAT | 2.3G CARBS | 0.4G SUGARS | 1.3G FIBER | 1.1G PROTEIN | 200MG SODIUM

SEAWEED AND SESAME SALAD

Seaweed is a fantastic source of minerals and fiber—and if you can find a bag of mixed seaweed, the variety of colors and textures is beautiful to look at.

SERVES: 2
PREP: 5 MINS, PLUS SOAKING

1 (3/4-ounce) package of mixed dried seaweed, soaked in water for 5–10 minutes
1 large scallion, finely chopped
1 red radish, finely chopped
2 teaspoons sesame seeds, to garnish

DRESSING
1 tablespoon cold-pressed extra virgin sesame oil
1 tablespoon raw rice vinegar
1 tablespoon raw coconut aminos sauce
1 teaspoon chopped red chile
2 teaspoons mirin (japanese rice wine) or sherry
1 teaspoon organic miso paste

1. While the seaweed mixture is soaking, make the dressing. Add the sesame oil, rice vinegar, coconut aminos sauce, chile, mirin, and miso paste to a screw-top jar or small bowl and shake or stir vigorously to combine.

2. Once the seaweed is tender and reconstituted, drain it thoroughly in a colander and rinse.

3. Divide the seaweed between two shallow bowls and drizzle the dressing over it, tossing lightly.

4. Sprinkle the chopped scallion and radish over the salad and garnish with the sesame seeds to serve.

ALL KINDS OF SEAWEED
Dried seaweed mixes are available in Asian grocery stores, health food stores, and online. Some kinds you can try are wakame, dulse, agar agar, miyoek, chondrus, and kelp.

PER SERVING: 137 CALS | 9.2G FAT | 1.4G SAT FAT | 8.2G CARBS | 2.5G SUGARS | 1.1G FIBER | 11.6G PROTEIN | 200MG SODIUM

OAT BREAD
WITH CHIA SEEDS

Following a raw diet doesn't mean giving up bread.
For a delicious and extremely nutritious snack, you can make
this oat, seed, and nut loaf flavored with green olives.

MAKES: 1 LOAF (AROUND 12 SLICES)
PREP: 10 MINS, PLUS SOAKING AND DEHYDRATING

⅔ cup raw rolled oats
⅔ cup raw oat flour
¾ cup plus 1 tablespoon buckwheat flour
⅓ cup pumpkin seeds
⅔ cup raw walnuts, ground
2 tablespoons psyllium husk powder
8 green olives, pitted and sliced
2 teaspoons sun-dried herbes de Provence
(or half-dried parsley and half-dried rosemary)
1 teaspoon sea salt
½ teaspoon black pepper
1 tablespoon cold-pressed extra virgin canola oil
2 tablespoons chia seeds, soaked in ½ cup water
for 20 minutes

1. You will need a dehydrator for this recipe. If you don't have a dehydrator, an electric oven may have a setting to dehydrate food on a low enough heat. It may be the defrost setting or slightly higher, or a designated dehydrate setting. Check you have the correct temperature with an oven thermometer before dehydrating in a standard oven.

2. Combine the oats, oat flour, buckwheat flour, pumpkin seeds, ground walnuts, and psyllium in a large mixing bowl. Stir in the olives, herbs, salt, pepper, and canola oil. Mix thoroughly.

3. Add the soaked chia seeds and their water to the mixing bowl and knead the mix. If the dough doesn't come together, add a tablespoon of water and knead again. Repeat if necessary. To make a fairly dry dough, ¼ cup of water should be enough.

4. On a board, form the dough into an oblong shape and transfer to a nonstick dehydrator sheet. (If using the oven, use a nonstick oven pan.) Using a sharp knife, score slices along the bread, cutting two-thirds of the way into the loaf.

5. Place the sheet on a dehydrator tray and dehydrate on high for an hour (140°F), then turn to low (115°F) and continue dehydrating for 6 hours. Cut slices along the scores you made and dehydrate for an additional hour on low, or until you have firm slices.

6. Store the oat bread in an airtight container.

SWAP THE NUTS
Walnuts provide a richness and depth of flavor,
but you can substitute them with ground
Brazil nuts or ground hazelnuts.

PER SLICE: 163 CALS | 9.3G FAT | 1.1G SAT FAT | 17.4G CARBS | 0.4G SUGARS | 5.4G FIBER | 5G PROTEIN | 240MG SODIUM

SEEDBURST FLATBREADS

These delicious, lightly dehydrated flatbreads are easy to make and are bursting with nuts, seeds, and an array of vegetables.

MAKES: 8 FLATBREADS
PREP: 10 MINS, PLUS DEHYDRATING

2 tablespoons milled flaxseed
2 tablespoons hulled hemp seeds
5 tablespoons sunflower seeds
2 tablespoons raw walnuts
1 tablespoon raw rolled oats
1 zucchini, peeled and coarsely chopped
1 small carrot, peeled and coarsely chopped
1 large celery stalk, chopped
3 baby corn
1 red bell pepper, chopped
1 tablespoon cold-pressed extra virgin canola oil
1 teaspoon sea salt

1. You will need a dehydrator for this recipe. If you don't have a dehydrator, an electric oven may have a setting to dehydrate food on a low enough heat. It may be the defrost setting or slightly higher, or a designated dehydrate setting. Check you have the correct temperature with an oven thermometer before dehydrating in a standard oven.

2. Put the flaxseed and hemp seeds in a mixing bowl with 3 tablespoons of the sunflower seeds.

3. Grind the rest of the sunflower seeds, the walnuts, and oats in a food processor and transfer to the mixing bowl. Add the zucchini, carrot, celery, and corn to the processor and pulse until they are finely chopped. Add the red bell pepper and pulse for 1–2 seconds.

4. Transfer the vegetable mixture to the bowl and stir in the canola oil and salt. Add 1–2 tablespoons of water if the mixture seems dry. Stir again.

5. Transfer the mixture to two nonstick dehydrator sheets on dehydrator trays and press down to about 1/4–3/8 inch thick. Dehydrate on high (140°F) for an hour, then turn to low (115°F) and dehydrate for an additional 2–3 hours, or until the flatbread feels fairly dry to the touch.

6. Flip the flatbread over with a large flat spatula and score with a sharp knife to make eight large squares. Dehydrate on low for an additional 2–3 hours, or until the mixture is dry but still has some give—you want flatbread, not crackers.

7. Break or cut the flatbreads along the scores you made. Let them cool completely, then store in an airtight container.

SERVING IDEA
Try a flatbread topped with slices of tomato and avocado, or raw cashew butter and cucumber.

PER FLATBREAD: 102 CALS | 8G FAT | 0.7G SAT FAT | 5.1G CARBS | 1.9G SUGARS | 2.2G FIBER | 3.3G PROTEIN | 320MG SODIUM

MAIN DISHES

CUCUMBER NOODLE BOWL WITH THAI DRESSING

This spicy Thai salad is a great source of cholesterol-lowering foods, such as beet, kale, and seaweed. It also features a delicious peanut topping for a healthy heart.

SERVES: 2
PREP: 15 MINS

1 beet, peeled and spiralized
½ cucumber, spiralized
1 cup chopped kale
½ red onion, thinly sliced
1 small carrot, peeled and thinly sliced
⅓ cup raw peanuts
2 teaspoon ground red seaweed
¼ cup fresh coconut flakes, to garnish
1 tablespoon fresh cilantro leaves, to garnish

DRESSING
2 tablespoons cold-pressed extra virgin sesame oil
2 teaspoons organic miso paste
juice of ½ lime
½-inch piece of fresh ginger, minced
1 large garlic clove, minced
1 small red chile, minced
2 teaspoons raw peanut butter
salt (optional)

1. Arrange all but a few strands of the beet in two serving bowls. Add all of the cucumber strands.

2. Add the kale to the bowls and top with the onion and carrot.

3. To make the dressing, combine all the ingredients in a small bowl and mix well. Spoon it over the beet salad.

4. Run the peanuts under cold water, then pat them dry so they are just slightly damp. On a plate, roll them in the seaweed until they are thoroughly coated, then sprinkle them over the salad.

5. Add the coconut flakes and cilantro leaves to the salad. Garnish with the remaining beet strands to serve.

NUTTY ADDITIONS
You can use raw peanut butter or raw cashew butter in the dressing and you can choose either of these nuts for the garnish.

PER SERVING: 409 CALS | 30.4G FAT | 6.7G SAT FAT | 29.1G CARBS | 12.1G SUGARS | 8.4G FIBER | 11.5G PROTEIN | 280MG SODIUM

CAULIFLOWER SALAD WITH APPLE AND NUTS

Raw cauliflower, with its mild, slightly nutty flavor, tastes wonderful mixed with crisp spirals of apple, a sprinkling of walnuts, and a fabulous tangy dressing.

SERVES: 4
PREP: 15 MINS

1 cauliflower, divided into small florets
1 large, red-skinned dessert apple,
such as Red Delicious, cored and chopped
2 tablespoons sunflower seeds
1 tablespoon sesame seeds
3 tablespoons chopped raw walnuts
1 large sweet potato, peeled and spiralized
1 small red onion, spiralized
1 tablespoon cold-pressed extra virgin canola oil
½ teaspoon sea salt
¼ teaspoon black pepper
2 teaspoon chopped fresh dill, to garnish

DRESSING
3 tablespoons raw coconut yogurt (see page 15)
juice of ½ lemon
2 teaspoons grated fresh horseradish
1 tablespoon chopped fresh dill
1 garlic clove, crushed
½ teaspoon sea salt
½ teaspoon black pepper

1. Put the cauliflower florets into a large bowl. Add three-quarters of the apple, all of the seeds, and 2 tablespoons of the walnuts.

2. Beat all the dressing ingredients together in a small bowl and pour it over the cauliflower mixture. Stir well until everything is coated.

3. Divide the sweet potato spirals among four serving dishes and sprinkle the onion spirals on top. Drizzle with the canola oil, then add the salt and pepper.

4. Spoon the cauliflower mixture into the serving dishes. Top with the remaining apple and walnuts, and garnish with the dill to serve.

PER SERVING: 263 CALS | 14.2G FAT | 3.6G SAT FAT | 30.8G CARBS | 12.4G SUGARS | 7.5G FIBER | 7.1G PROTEIN | 680MG SODIUM

RAW VEGETABLE LASAGNE

With there being several layers in this wonderful raw lasagne, you might think it's a lot of work—however, it is easy to put together and is ideal for a dinner party.

SERVES: 2
PREP: 1HR 30 MINS

ZUCCHINI LAYER
1 zucchini, thinly sliced lengthwise
1½ teaspoons olive oil
2 teaspoons balsamic vinegar
¼ teaspoon salt

NUT CHEESE LAYER
⅔ cup shelled macadamia nuts
½ small yellow bell pepper, diced
1 tablespoon nutritional yeast flakes
1½ tablespoons lemon juice
¼ teaspoon salt

TOMATO SAUCE
2 tablespoons tomato paste
½ teaspoon garlic paste
¼ teaspoon smoked paprika
½ teaspoon salt (optional)

AVOCADO PESTO
⅓ cup pine nuts
1 large ripe avocado, coarsely chopped
3 tablespoons fresh basil leaves
1 small garlic clove, crushed
juice of ½ lime
¼ teaspoon salt

TOMATO AND SPINACH
2 large tomatoes, sliced
1 cup baby spinach leaves, trimmed
2 teaspoons pine nuts, toasted, to garnish
2 teaspoons basil leaves, to garnish

1. To make the zucchini layer, place the zucchini in a dish that will hold the slices in one layer. Cover the slices with the oil, vinegar, and salt, making sure that each slice is well covered, then set aside for up to 1 hour to soften and absorb the flavors.

2. To make the cheese layer, pulse all the ingredients in a blender until you have a smooth, light paste.

3. To make the tomato sauce, combine all the ingredients in a small bowl, then add about 2 tablespoons of cold water and mix thoroughly. Add a little more water until you have a pouring consistency. Add salt, if using.

4. To make the avocado pesto layer, put the pine nuts into an electric mini chopper or blender and process for a few seconds, or until chopped but not pureed. Add the avocado chunks, basil leaves, garlic, lime juice, and salt and pulse until you have a lightly textured mixture. Slice the tomatoes so that you have six inside slices from each. Discard the outer slices.

5. Layer the two lasagne servings directly onto plates. Arrange one-quarter of the zucchini slices in a rectangle on the center of each plate. For each plate, top with one-quarter of the spinach leaves, then spoon one-quarter of the nut cheese over them. Add one-quarter of the tomato slices and top them with one-quarter of the avocado pesto. For each plate, add another one-quarter of the tomato slices, one-quarter of the cheese, one-quarter of the spinach, and one-quarter of the avocado pesto. Finish by placing the remaining zucchini slices on top of each lasagne.

6. Drizzle the sauce over the two lasagne and garnish with toasted pine nuts and basil leaves.

PER SERVING: 799 CALS | 72.6G FAT | 9.9G SAT FAT | 37.8G CARBS | 14.1G SUGARS | 16.5G FIBER | 15.1G PROTEIN | 920MG SODIUM

AVOCADO HERO SALAD

This salad is full of gorgeous textures, contrasting creamy avocado with crunchy asparagus tips, and it is rich in heart-healthy monounsaturated fats, soluble fiber, and vitamin E.

SERVES: 2
PREP: 10 MINS, PLUS SPROUTING

½ cup dry green peas suitable for sprouting
½ cup whole quinoa seeds suitable for sprouting
2½ cups baby spinach
2½ ounces baby asparagus tips
16 baby plum tomatoes
1 cup fresh watercress
2 ripe avocados, pitted, peeled, and sliced into bite-size pieces
2 tablespoons raw pine nuts
8 fresh basil sprigs
1½ teaspoons cold-pressed extra virgin olive oil

DRESSING

2 tablespoons cold-pressed extra virgin olive oil
1½ teaspoons raw wine vinegar
2 teaspoons raw honey
1 teaspoon stone-ground mustard
½ teaspoon sea salt
½ teaspoon pepper

1. To sprout the peas, put them into a wide-neck glass jar and soak overnight in lukewarm water, covered with cheesecloth or a similar material. In the morning, drain and rinse the peas and fill the jar with fresh water. Drain and rinse the peas twice a day for five days, until they sprout. Rinse and drain to use.

2. To sprout the quinoa, use the same method as the peas but soak them for only 4 hours. They will sprout in about two days.

3. Arrange the spinach, all but four of the asparagus tips, and the plum tomatoes in two serving dishes with most of the watercress.

4. Arrange three-quarters of the avocado slices in the dishes with the remaining watercress and the pea and quinoa sprouts. Sprinkle three-quarters of the pine nuts on top.

5. In a small bowl, mash the remaining avocado with the remaining pine nuts, six of the basil sprigs, and the olive oil until you have a coarse puree.

6. Make the dressing by thoroughly combining the ingredients in a small dish. Spoon most of it over the salad.

7. Finish the salad by arranging two asparagus tips in the center of each dish, followed by half the avocado puree and a basil sprig. Drizzle with the rest of the dressing to serve.

WHY NOT TRY?
You can use slivered almonds or chopped hazelnuts if you don't have any pine nuts.

PER SERVING: 813 CALS | 48.5G FAT | 6.2G SAT FAT | 80.6G CARBS | 13.3G SUGARS | 27.1G FIBER | 23.4G PROTEIN | 640MG SODIUM

FRUIT AND VEGETABLE KABOBS

When you want something fresh, zingy, and packed with vitamin C and antioxidants, these kabobs are the perfect meal.

SERVES: 4
PREP: 10 MINS, PLUS MARINATING

1 small Florence fennel bulb, divided into leaves
1 small turnip, peeled and thinly sliced
1/16 butternut squash, peeled and thinly sliced
1 yellow bell pepper, seeded and cut into squares
1 papaya, peeled, seeded, and cut into cubes
1/2 mango, peeled and cut into chunks
8 prepared fresh coconut chunks

MARINADE

2 tablespoons cold-pressed extra virgin olive oil
2 teaspoon raw agave nectar
2 tablespoons orange juice
1 tablespoon raw coconut aminos sauce
1/2 teaspoon sea salt
1/2 teaspoon black pepper

SALAD

4 1/2 cups fresh herb and salad greens, such as sorrel, mizuna, flat-leaf parsley, cilantro, and celery
2 teaspoons poppy seeds
2 tablespoons raw coconut yogurt
1/3 cup raw coconut milk
1 tablespoon raw apple cider vinegar
1 garlic clove, crushed
1/2 teaspoon sea salt

1. You will need four wooden skewers for this recipe.

2. To make the kabobs, put all the fruit and vegetables into a nonmetallic dish and mix well.

3. In a small bowl, combine the marinade ingredients, then pour them over the kabob mixture. Stir well, cover, and set aside for 3–5 hours.

4. Shake any excess marinade off the fruit and vegetables, and thread them onto four wooden skewers.

5. Arrange the salad greens on four serving plates and sprinkle with the poppy seeds. Combine the yogurt, coconut milk, vinegar, garlic, and salt in a separate small bowl and drizzle the dressing over the salad.

6. Serve the kabobs alongside the salad.

TURNIP SUBSTITUTIONS
If you can find it, salsify or daikon (Japanese white radish) make great alternatives to the turnip.

PER SERVING: 285 CALS | 18.8G FAT | 10.7G SAT FAT | 29.3G CARBS | 18.6G SUGARS | 7.4G FIBER | 3.5G PROTEIN | 640MG SODIUM

SEAWEED POWER BOWL

Seaweed is an extraordinary source of a nutrient missing in almost every other food—iodine. This is critically important to maintaining a healthy thyroid. A small serving of seaweed just once a week is recommended.

SERVES: 4
PREP: 20 MINS

¼ ounce dried kelp
or dried kombu
½ cucumber
2 oranges
1 red chile, seeded and finely diced
2 carrots, grated
1 large mango, peeled, pitted, and chopped
3 heads of bok choy, chopped
½ ounce fresh cilantro leaves
2 tablespoons chopped salted peanuts

DRESSING
3 tablespoons olive oil
grated zest and juice of 1 lime
1 teaspoon honey
1 teaspoon miso paste

1. Put the kelp into a bowl of water and let stand for 10 minutes to rehydrate.

2. Meanwhile, to make the dressing, whisk together the oil, lime zest and juice, honey, and miso paste.

3. Halve the cucumber lengthwise and, using a teaspoon, scoop out and discard the seeds.

4. Peel the oranges and cut them into sections.

5. Coarsely chop the kelp and put into a large bowl with the cucumber, orange sections, chile, carrot, mango, bok choy, and half the mint and cilantro.

6. Pour in the dressing and toss well. Divide among four bowls.

7. Sprinkle each bowl with chopped peanuts and the remaining mint and cilantro.

WHY NOT TRY?

If you can't find dried kelp or kombu, substitute it with nori sheets, which can be served dry, broken into shards, to add an extra crunch to the salad.

PER SERVING: 259 CALS | 13.5G FAT | 1.9G SAT FAT | 32G CARBS | 22.2G SUGARS | 7.4G FIBER | 5.3G PROTEIN | 160MG SODIUM

SWEET-AND-SOUR "STIR-FRY"

This attractive, Asian-inspired bowl is filled with goodies—raw kelp noodles are low in carbs and calories, and Asian mushrooms can help regulate the immune system.

SERVES: 2
PREP: 15 MINS, PLUS SPROUTING AND SOAKING

¼ cup adzuki beans suitable for sprouting
¼ cup mung beans suitable for sprouting
1 parsnip, peeled and coarsely chopped
1 small sweet potato, peeled and coarsely chopped
1½ tablespoons dried shiitake mushrooms, soaked in water for 15 minutes, drained, and rinsed
7 ounces raw kelp noodles
¾ cup sliced bok choy
1¾ ounces enoki mushrooms
1 mild red chile, seeded and finely sliced
¼ cup raw pine nuts

CHILI SAUCE

1 small, medium-hot red chile, seeded and chopped
1 teaspoon peeled and chopped fresh ginger
1 tablespoon raw coconut aminos sauce
2 teaspoons raw agave nectar
1 tablespoon cold-pressed extra virgin sesame oil
1 teaspoon raw tahini
juice of ½ lime
2 teaspoons raw rice vinegar

1. Start sprouting the adzuki and mung beans three days before you want to make the stir-fry. Put the beans into a wide-neck glass jar and soak them overnight in lukewarm water, covered with cheesecloth or a similar material. In the morning, drain and rinse the beans and fill the jar with fresh water. Drain and rinse them twice a day for three days, until they sprout. Rinse and drain to use.

2. To make the stir-fry sauce, process all the ingredients until you have a paste. Add a little water until you have a thick pouring consistency and stir well.

3. Put the parsnip into a food processor and process until you have rice-size pieces. Transfer to a mixing bowl. Do the same with the sweet potato and then lightly mix the two vegetables.

4. Chop the soaked shiitake mushrooms into small pieces and mix them into the vegetable rice.

5. Rinse the kelp noodles and shake to dry in a strainer. Arrange most of them in two serving bowls and top with the vegetable rice mixture.

6. Arrange the bok choy and enoki mushrooms on top of the rice, then dot spoonfuls of the sauce around the dish.

7. Finish with the chile slices, pine nuts, and bean sprouts. Finally, arrange the few remaining kelp noodles on top and serve.

RICE ALTERNATIVES
You can use cauliflower instead of the parsnip to make your rice, and you can vary the type of seed sprouts you use. Lentil and chickpea sprouts are great alternatives.

PER SERVING: 489 CALS | 19.2G FAT | 2G SAT FAT | 69.2G CARBS | 14.8G SUGARS | 14.1G FIBER | 12.5G PROTEIN | 120MG SODIUM

RAW SHOOTS AND SEEDS SUPER SALAD

Raw shoots and seeds are superfoods because the sprouting process increases the proportion of protein and fiber within each seedling, and gives them a lower glycemic index. They are always best eaten fresh.

SERVES: 6
PREP: 20 MINUTES

2–3 cups mixed seed and bean sprouts
(such as alfalfa, mung beans, soybeans, adzuki beans, chickpeas, and radish seeds)
3 tablespoons pumpkin seeds
3 tablespoons sunflower seeds
3 tablespoons sesame seeds
1 small Pippin apple
½ cup dried apricots
grated zest and juice of 1 lemon
½ cup walnuts, coarsely chopped
2 tablespoons vegan omega-rich oil

1. In a large mixing bowl, combine the sprouts and seeds. Core and chop the apple and chop the apricots into small pieces. Stir the fruit into the bowl, then stir in the lemon zest and walnuts.

2. Make a dressing by mixing the lemon juice with the oil in a small bowl, using a fork to thoroughly combine.

3. Stir the dressing into the salad and serve immediately.

SPROUTING
Lentils, peas, adzuki beans, mung beans, and chickpeas are easy to sprout—sprouting will take four to eight days. Only consume them after they sprout, when the natural toxins have broken down.

Note: recipes using bean sprouts should be avoided by children younger than five, older adults, pregnant women, and those with weakened immune systems, who are particularly vulnerable to the bacteria that may be present.

PER SERVING: 252 CALS | 19.1G FAT | 2G SAT FAT | 17.5G CARBS | 9.8G SUGARS | 4G FIBER | 8.4G PROTEIN | TRACE SODIUM

RAW PIZZA

Sometimes all you want after a busy week is pizza. Unlike greasy fast-food pizza, this version is much healthier, with a delectable nutty base and a mouthwatering spinach spreading sauce.

MAKES: 2 (8-INCH) PIZZAS TO SERVE 4
PREP: 30 MINS, PLUS DEHYDRATING AND MARINATING

PIZZA CRUST

1/2 cup raw walnuts
1/3 cup sunflower seeds
1/4 cup pumpkin seeds
1 cup hulled hemp seeds
1/4 cup milled flaxseed
3/4 cup buckwheat flour
1/2 teaspoon sea salt and 1/2 teaspoon black pepper
1 celery stalk, chopped, and 1 small onion, chopped
1 tablespoon water, plus extra if necessary

SPINACH SPREADING SAUCE

1 cup small spinach leaves, chopped
3/4 cup fresh basil leaves
1/4 cup raw pine nuts
2 garlic cloves, crushed
1/2 teaspoon sea salt and 1 teaspoon black pepper
2 tablespoons cold-pressed extra virgin olive oil

TOPPINGS

6 cremini mushrooms, sliced
1/2 red onion, thinly sliced
12 baby spinach leaves
2 tomatoes, sliced
8 cherry tomatoes, halved
pinch black pepper, to serve

MARINADE

2 tablespoons cold-pressed extra virgin olive oil
1 1/2 teaspoons raw apple cider vinegar
2 teaspoons raw coconut aminos
1/2 teaspoon black pepper

1. You will need a dehydrator for this recipe. If you don't have a dehydrator, an electric oven may have a setting to dehydrate food on a low enough heat. It may be the defrost setting or slightly higher, or a designated dehydrate setting. Check you have the correct temperature with an oven thermometer before dehydrating in a standard oven.

2. To make the pizza crust, pulse the walnuts, sunflower seeds, and pumpkin seeds in a food processor for a few seconds, until coarsely ground. Transfer to a mixing bowl with the hemp seeds, flaxseed, buckwheat flour, salt, and pepper, and stir.

3. Add the celery and onion to the processor and pulse to a puree, then spoon into the mixing bowl. Add the tablespoon of water and mix everything together, adding a little more water and mixing again until you have a fairly dry dough.

4. Shape the dough into two 8-inch circles on nonstick dehydrator sheets. (If using the oven, use a nonstick oven pan.) Dehydrate for 3 hours on low (115°F), then turn the crusts over and dehydrate for an additional 3 hours on low, or until lightly crisped and firm.

5. Meanwhile, start preparing the toppings. Put the mushrooms and onion into a shallow nonmetallic dish. Mix the marinade ingredients together and pour into the dish, making sure all the vegetables are coated. Cover and let stand for 2 hours to soften and absorb the flavors.

6. To make the spinach sauce, put all the ingredients into a mortar and pound with a pestle. For a smoother spread, you can process the ingredients in a food processor.

7. Spread half the sauce over each pizza crust and divide the topping ingredients between each one. Drizzle a little marinade over the pizzas and grind black pepper over the top to serve.

PER SERVING: 670 CALS | 50G FAT | 5.5G SAT FAT | 36.1G CARBS | 5.6G SUGARS | 11.8G FIBER | 25.6G PROTEIN | 640MG SODIUM

FALAFEL WITH RAW HUMMUS

Falafel is a popular Middle Eastern dish that's usually deep-fried. This healthy, but just as tasty, raw version is made from chickpea sprouts and sweet potato, perfect for serving with the homemade hummus.

SERVES: 4

PREP: 20 MINS, PLUS SPROUTING AND DEHYDRATING

1 cup chickpeas suitable for sprouting
1 sweet potato, peeled and coarsely chopped
1 tablespoon milled flaxseed
1 tablespoon raw light tahini
1 teaspoon ground cumin seeds
1 small medium-hot red chile, seeded
2 teaspoons peeled and chopped fresh ginger
2 teaspoons raw coconut aminos sauce
1 tablespoon chopped fresh parsley
1 tablespoon chopped fresh cilantro leaves
2 tablespoons sesame seeds
sea salt (optional)
black pepper (optional)

RAW HUMMUS
1 zucchini, peeled and coarsely chopped
1 tablespoon raw light tahini
juice of ½ lemon
2 garlic cloves, crushed
½ teaspoon ground cumin seeds
¼ teaspoon sea salt

SALAD
1 small carrot, peeled and sliced
½ red bell pepper, seeded and sliced
12 Boston or small butter lettuce leaves
8 radishes, sliced
4 teaspoons cold-pressed extra virgin olive oil

1. You will need a dehydrator for this recipe. If you don't have a dehydrator, an electric oven may have a setting to dehydrate food on a low enough heat. It may be the defrost setting or slightly higher, or a designated dehydrate setting. Check you have the correct temperature with an oven thermometer before dehydrating in a standard oven.

2. Start sprouting the chickpeas three to five days before making the recipe. Put the chickpeas into a jar and cover with lukewarm water. Keep in a warm, dark room. Soak for 24 hours, then drain and rinse, and drain again. Rinse and drain twice a day for three to five days. When the sprouts are about ⅜ inch long, they are ready.

3. Process the chickpeas and sweet potato in a food processor until you have a fairly smooth but lightly textured mix.

4. Add the flaxseed, tahini, cumin seeds, chile, ginger, and coconut aminos sauce to the processor and blend to combine. Transfer the mixture to a bowl and stir in the parsley and cilantro. Season with salt and pepper, if using.

5. Mold the mixture into 20 small balls and roll them in the sesame seeds. Transfer to a nonstick dehydrator sheet on a dehydrator tray. (If using the oven, use a nonstick oven pan.) Dehydrate on low (115°F) for 6 hours, then turn them over and dehydrate on low for an additional 2 hours.

6. To make the salad, mix the vegetables together in a serving bowl and drizzle with the olive oil.

7. To make the hummus, put all the ingredients into a clean processor and blend until you have a fairly smooth mix. Serve the falafels alongside the dip and the salad.

> Note: sprouted chickpeas should be avoided by children younger than five, older adults, pregnant women, and those with weakened immune systems.

PER SERVING: 381 CALS | 14.9G FAT | 1.9G SAT FAT | 51G CARBS | 10.5G SUGARS | 11.3G FIBER | 14.7G PROTEIN | 200MG SODIUM

SPAGHETTI WITH GARLIC CREAM SAUCE AND BABY TOMATOES

It's so easy to make raw spaghetti if you own a spiralizer—this carb-free version creates strands of pasta from zucchini and is topped with a velvety garlic sauce.

SERVES: 2
PREP: 20 MINS, PLUS SOAKING

2 zucchini, spiralized
1 tablespoon cold-pressed extra virgin olive oil
½ teaspoon sea salt

GARLIC CREAM SAUCE

²/₃ cup raw skinned almonds, soaked in water for
2 hours, drained and rinsed
2 tablespoons raw almond milk
1 large garlic clove, chopped
1 scallion, chopped
2 teaspoons raw apple cider vinegar
½ teaspoon sea salt

TO SERVE

6 sun-dried tomato pieces
10 baby plum tomatoes, halved
1 scallion, chopped
2 fresh basil sprigs, leaves separated

1. To make the garlic cream sauce, pulse the soaked almonds in a food processor until they are ground. Add the almond milk, garlic, scallion, vinegar, and salt, then blend until you have a thick, creamy paste. Transfer to a bowl.

2. Toss the zucchini spirals in the olive oil and salt. Divide the spirals between two serving bowls.

3. Spoon the creamy sauce into the center of each bowl, then top with the sun-dried tomatoes, plum tomatoes, scallions, and basil leaves. Serve immediately.

SPAGHETTI OPTIONS

Try different vegetables for your 'spaghetti' as the seasons pass—summer squash is ideal in summer and butternut squash is great in winter.

PER SERVING: 428 CALS | 35.2G FAT | 3.1G SAT FAT | 21.4G CARBS | 9.9G SUGARS | 8.4G FIBER | 14.7G PROTEIN | 600MG SODIUM

GADO GADO SALAD

Tossing raw cauliflower and broccoli with crunchy bean sprouts and cucumber and coating them with an Indonesian toasted peanut and soy dressing turns everyday ingredients into something exotic and good for you.

SERVES: 4
PREP: 10–15 MINS

¼ head cauliflower, cored and cut into small florets
1½ cups small broccoli florets
1 cup shredded savoy cabbage
1½ cups bean sprouts
1 cucumber, peeled, halved lengthwise, seeded, and thickly sliced
1 red bell pepper, halved, seeded, and finely chopped

DRESSING
2 tablespoons peanut oil
¾ cup unsalted peanuts, finely chopped
2 garlic cloves, minced
2 tablespoons soy sauce
juice of 2 limes
½ red chile, seeded and minced

1. Put the cauliflower, broccoli, cabbage, bean sprouts, cucumber, and red bell pepper into a salad bowl and toss gently together.

2. To make the dressing, warm 1 tablespoon of the oil in a pan over medium heat (you can warm raw food below a temperature of 104°F). Add the peanuts and garlic and warm for 2—3 minutes and then remove from the heat and stir in the soy sauce, lime juice, chile, and remaining oil, then leave at room temperature for a couple of hours.

3. When ready to eat, mix the dressing thoroughly, spoon the dressing over the salad and toss them gently together. Spoon into four bowls, then serve immediately.

MUNG BEAN SPROUTS
Mung bean sprouts, widely available in supermarkets all year round, are a good addition to this recipe. Low in calories, they also have fiber, B vitamins, and vitamins C and K.

PER SERVING: 259 CALS | 17.8G FAT | 2.6G SAT FAT | 19.9G CARBS | 7.7G SUGARS | 6.6G FIBER | 10.2G PROTEIN | 40MG SODIUM

DESSERTS AND SWEET TREATS

PEACH AND ORANGE GRANITA

A fruity Italian granita makes a quick and refreshingly light dessert.
By using fruit pulp instead of just juice, you also get plenty of fiber and vitamin C.

SERVES: 4
PREP: 10 MINS, PLUS FREEZING

juice of 2 large oranges
4 peaches, pitted and peeled
juice of 1 lime
3 tablespoons raw agave nectar
seeds from ½ vanilla bean
1 orange, cut into slices, to decorate
4 fresh mint leaves, to decorate

1. Put the orange juice, peaches, lime juice, agave nectar, and vanilla seeds into a blender and blend until smooth or until a few small peach pieces are left.

2. Pour the mixture into a shallow, freeze-proof container, cover with a lid, and freeze for 2 hours.

3. Stir the mixture with a fork, bringing the frozen edges into the center. Replace the lid and freeze for another 2 hours.

4. Stir again and freeze for another hour, or until nearly frozen in the center. Stir again before dividing the granita among four glasses. Serve decorated with the orange slices and mint leaves.

FRUIT FAVORITES
You can try the same recipe using 1 large ripe mango, 2 papayas, or 4 nectarines instead of the peach.

PER SERVING: 142 CALS | 0.5G FAT | TRACE SAT FAT | 34.9G CARBS | 30.6G SUGARS | 3.2G FIBER | 2G PROTEIN | TRACE SODIUM

MIXED FRUIT
SOUP BOWL

This summery cold fruit soup is perfect for a hot day, and it is rich in antioxidants from its beautiful bright colors. Papaya is also a rich source of proteolytic enzymes, mainly papain, which greatly aid the digestive process.

SERVES: 4
PREP: 15 MINS, PLUS CHILLING

2 papaya, peeled, seeded, and chopped
2 cups hulled strawberries
1 honeydew melon, seeded, peeled, and chopped
1/3 cup fresh mint leaves
1 tablespoon preserved ginger syrup
1 preserved ginger
2/3 cup blueberries

1. Reserving 1 tablespoon of the chopped papaya, put the remainder into a food processor with $1^3/_4$ cups of the strawberries and process to a smooth puree.

2. Pour into a small bowl and chill in the refrigerator for 10 minutes.

3. Put all but 1 tablespoon of the chopped melon into the food processor with half the mint leaves, the ginger syrup, and preserved ginger. Process to a smooth puree. Pour into a small bowl and chill in the refrigerator for 10 minutes.

4. When you are ready to serve, divide each soup among four bowls, then use a knife to swirl them together. Drop a couple of ice cubes into each bowl.

5. Dice the reserved fruits and sprinkle them over the soup, together with the blueberries and remaining mint leaves.

FRUITS OF CHANGE
When possible, use fruits that are in season. This is also delicious made with raspberries instead of strawberries, and is just as healthy.

PER SERVING: 173 CALS | 0.9G FAT | 0.2G SAT FAT | 43.1G CARBS | 34.4G SUGARS | 5.7G FIBER | 2.2G PROTEIN | 40MG SODIUM

CACAO AND AVOCADO MOUSSE WITH CINNAMON BERRIES

Here's an unusual dessert that you definitely do not have to feel guilty for enjoying—it is full of healthy ingredients and sweetened with agave nectar instead of sugar.

SERVES: 4
PREP: 4 HRS 15 MINS

2 ripe avocados, halved and pitted
²/₃ cup cacao powder
¼ cup agave nectar
seeds from ½ vanilla bean
½ teaspoon chili powder
¼ cup coconut milk
⅓ cup hulled wild strawberries
or hulled small strawberries
⅓ cup fresh raspberries
½ teaspoon ground cinnamon

1. Scoop the avocado flesh into a large bowl and mash lightly with a fork. Stir in the cacao powder, agave nectar, vanilla seeds, and chili powder. Blend thoroughly with an immersion blender until the mixture is thick and smooth. Stir in the coconut milk and blend again.

2. Spoon the avocado mixture into ramekins (individual ceramic dishes) or small, stemmed glasses. Cover with plastic wrap and chill for at least 4 hours.

3. Decorate the avocado mousses evenly with the berries and sprinkle the cinnamon over each dish. Serve immediately.

CACAO RICHNESS
Cacao is rich in antioxidants, including flavonoids and catechins—its antioxidant level is higher even than green and black tea, and cacao is also packed with fiber.

PER SERVING: 249 CALS | 15.8G FAT | 5.1G SAT FAT | 32.9G CARBS | 17G SUGARS | 11.7G FIBER | 4.9G PROTEIN | TRACE SODIUM

LAYERED APPLE PIE

This raw apple pie is a delicious, contemporary twist on a beloved classic. With its magical layers of apple, dates, and spices, it tastes even better than the original.

SERVES: 8
PREP: 20 MINS, PLUS SOAKING, FREEZING AND CHILLING

1½ cups raw walnuts
4 Medjool dates, pitted
2 tablespoons melted cold-pressed extra virgin coconut oil
8 Medjool dates, pitted, soaked in water for 4 hours, drained, and rinsed
1 small banana, peeled and coarsely chopped
1 apple, such as Red Delicious, Pink Lady, or Fuji, peeled, cored and coarsely chopped
1 teaspoon ground cinnamon
½ teaspoon ground nutmeg
1 teaspoon seeds from 1 vanilla bean
½ teaspoon sea salt
juice of ½ lemon
5 sweet, crisp apples, such as Red Delicious, Pink Lady, or Fuji, cored
⅓ cup golden raisins
½ teaspoon ground cinnamon, for dusting

1. Line an 8 x 2½-inch round cake pan with nonstick parchment paper. Set aside.

2. To make the pie crust, pulse the walnuts in a food processor for a few seconds, then add the dates and process again until you have a fine, sticky mixture. Add the coconut oil and blend again.

3. Spoon the mixture into the prepared pan. Press down thoroughly and evenly, and put into the freezer to set for 1½–2 hours.

4. To make the filling, put the soaked dates, banana, and chopped apple into a clean food processor with the cinnamon, nutmeg, vanilla seeds, and salt. Pulse to thoroughly combine, then spoon into a mixing bowl.

5. Stir the lemon juice into a bowl of cold water. Using a mandoline slicer or sharp knife, thinly slice the dessert apples, adding them to the water bowl as you work (the acid from the lemon stops them from turning brown).

6. Spoon a thin layer of the filling onto the chilled pie crust and top with a few of the golden raisins and a layer of sliced apples. Push the apple slices down well. Repeat until you have used all the filling, sliced apples, and golden raisins, then dust the top of the pie with the cinnamon. Chill in the refrigerator for an hour before serving.

VARIATION
You can make a similar pie using firm dessert pears, such as Bartlett, instead of apples.

PER SERVING: 375 CALS | 18.4G FAT | 4.4G SAT FAT | 56.2G CARBS | 43.2G SUGARS | 7.6G FIBER | 4.8G PROTEIN | TRACE SODIUM

RAW BANANA, PINEAPPLE, AND PEANUT PIE

Here's a raw version of a tempting banana and caramel pie—made even better by adding pineapple and peanut butter. It's rich and smooth, with a gorgeous mixed nut crust.

SERVES: 8
PREP: 15 MINS, PLUS SOAKING AND FREEZING

PIE CRUST
1 cup raw hazelnuts
1 cup raw Brazil nuts
1 cup raw pecans
4 Medjool dates, pitted and chopped
1½ tablespoons maple syrup
2 tablespoons melted cold-pressed extra virgin coconut oil
1 tablespoon water

FILLING
4 ripe bananas, chopped
¼ cup raw peanut butter
3 slices ripe pineapple, chopped
1½ tablespoons melted raw unsweetened creamed coconut
½ teaspoon sea salt

TOPPING
1 banana, sliced and soaked in
¼ cup pineapple juice for 30 minutes
2 thin slices pineapple, chopped, to decorate
8 raw pecan halves, to decorate

1. Line an 8 x 2½-inch round cake pan with nonstick parchment paper. Set aside.

2. To make the pie crust, put all the nuts into a food processor and pulse for a few seconds. Add the dates, maple syrup, coconut oil, and water. Process until you have a crumbly, fairly fine mixture.

3. Press the nut mixture evenly and firmly into the prepared pan. Chill in the freezer for 2 hours.

4. Meanwhile, make the filling. Put all the ingredients into a food processor and process until the mixture is thoroughly blended. Spoon the filling onto the frozen crust and smooth the top. Freeze again for an hour or until the filling is firm.

5. To make the topping, arrange the soaked banana slices over the pie with the pineapple pieces and pecan halves. Keep the pie in the refrigerator until ready to serve.

GRATE THE GARNISH
Grate some raw cacao nibs over the top of the pie just before serving.

PER SERVING: 501 CALS | 37.4G FAT | 9.6G SAT FAT | 42.1G CARBS | 25.8G SUGARS | 7.6G FIBER | 8.7G PROTEIN | 160MG SODIUM

CHOCOLATE-AVOCADO LIME PIE

*With its nutty crust, luscious avocado filling, and chocolate topping,
this pie is true decadence—but because it's packed with vital nutrients,
healthy fats, and fiber, it's actually good for you.*

SERVES: 8
PREP: 30 MINS, PLUS SOAKING AND CHILLING

5 Medjool dates, pitted and coarsely chopped
½ cup raw macadamia nuts
⅔ cup raw pecans
20 raw Brazil nuts
1 tablespoon raw agave nectar
1 tablespoon melted cold-pressed
extra virgin coconut oil

AVOCADO FILLING

1½ cups raw cashew nuts, soaked in water for 4 hours,
drained, and rinsed
1¾ cups shredded fresh white coconut meat
2 tablespoons plus 2 teaspoons melted raw unsweetened
creamed coconut
2 ripe avocados, peeled, pitted, and coarsely chopped
juice of 2 limes
1 tablespoon melted cold-pressed
extra virgin coconut oil
¼ cup raw agave nectar

CHOCOLATE TOPPING

½ cup raw cashew nuts
2 tablespoons raw cacao powder
1 tablespoon melted cold-pressed
extra virgin coconut oil
¼ cup melted raw unsweetened creamed coconut
¼ cup raw agave nectar
1 tablespoon water
⅓ cup fresh white coconut meat shavings, to decorate

1. Line an 8-inch round cake pan with nonstick parchment paper and set aside.

2. Put the dates into a small bowl and soak for 10 minutes in enough warm water to cover. Drain and reserve the soaking water.

3. To make the pie crust, pulse the macadamia nuts, pecans, and Brazil nuts in a food processor for 10 seconds, then add the soaked dates and pulse again until everything is finely chopped. Add the agave nectar, soaking water, and coconut oil, then pulse again.

4. Press the mixture into the prepared pan and chill in the refrigerator for 2 hours, until firm.

5. To make the avocado filling, pulse the soaked cashew nuts in a clean food processor until you have a creamy puree. Transfer to a mixing bowl. Process the coconut meat to a paste, adding as little of the creamed coconut as necessary. Add the coconut to the mixing bowl.

6. Add the avocados to the processor with the lime juice, and pulse to a puree. Transfer to the mixing bowl. Stir in the rest of the creamed coconut, the coconut oil, and the agave nectar. Combine everything thoroughly.

7. Spread the filling over the firm crust and smooth the top. Chill in the refrigerator for another 2 hours.

8. Meanwhile, make the chocolate topping. Cream the cashew nuts as before and transfer to a small mixing bowl. Stir in the rest of the ingredients, reserving the coconut shavings for decoration.

9. When the filling is cool and firm, spread or pipe the topping over the pie. Decorate with the coconut shavings and chill until ready to serve.

PER SERVING: 784 CALS | 63.8G FAT | 27.2G SAT FAT | 52.9G CARBS | 32.3G SUGARS | 11.3G FIBER | 12G PROTEIN | TRACE SODIUM

CREAMY FIG SQUARES

These elegant fig squares are impressive to look at but easy to make. They're made with a high-fiber selection of fruit and nuts, then topped with a sweet almond cream.

MAKES: 9 SQUARES
PREP: 20 MINS, PLUS SOAKING AND FREEZING

8 moist sun-dried figs
3 Medjool dates, pitted
½ cup raw walnuts
12 raw Brazil nuts
2 tablespoons milled flaxseed
1½ teaspoons melted cold-pressed extra virgin coconut oil

TOPPING

⅓ cup plus 1 tablespoon raw almonds, soaked in water for 4 hours, drained, and rinsed
½ cup raw almond milk
2 tablespoons raw coconut flour
1½ tablespoons raw agave nectar
1 teaspoon seeds from 1 vanilla bean
1 tablespoon melted cold-pressed extra virgin coconut oil
5 fresh figs
2 fresh figs, sliced, to decorate

1. Line a 7-inch baking pan with nonstick parchment paper and set aside.

2. Put the sun-dried figs, dates, nuts, flaxseed, and coconut oil into a food processor and pulse until you have a crumbly, sticky mixture. Press into the prepared pan and freeze for 1–2 hours, until firm.

3. To make the topping, rub the skins off the soaked almonds—they should come away easily—and put them into a clean food processor, reserving five almonds for decoration. Pulse until you have a thick, creamy puree, then add the almond milk, coconut flour, agave nectar, vanilla seeds, and coconut oil. Blend again.

4. Scoop the flesh out of the five fresh figs and mash them with a fork in a small bowl. Stir them into the topping mixture.

5. Smooth the topping over the frozen mixture and freeze again for 1–2 hours. When firm, cut into squares and top each square with a slice of fresh fig. Chop the five reserved almonds and put a little on each fig slice. Serve the squares chilled.

PARTY SNACKS
Cut each square into four small bites and serve them as snacks at a dinner party.

PER SQUARE: 242 CALS | 16.1G FAT | 4G SAT FAT | 23.9G CARBS | 17.9G SUGARS | 5G FIBER | 4.9G PROTEIN | TRACE SODIUM

ALMOND AND BERRY PICK-ME-UP BARS

If you're feeling hungry between meals or your energy has dipped, one of these chocolate- and coconut-infused, nutrient-packed treats will pick you right up.

MAKES: 10 BARS
PREP: 15 MINS, PLUS SOAKING AND DEHYDRATING

½ cup pumpkin seeds
⅓ cup plus 1 tablespoon sunflower seeds
¾ cup plus 2 tablespoons raw almonds, soaked in water for 4 hours, drained, and rinsed
⅓ cup milled flaxseed
¼ cup raw agave nectar
1½ teaspoons ground cinnamon
⅓ cup dried goji berries, soaked in water for 30 minutes, drained, and rinsed
½ cup cacao nibs
2 tablespoons chopped goldenberries
1 tablespoon sesame seeds
1½ tablespoons buckwheat flour
1½ tablespoons raw unsweetened creamed coconut

CHOCOLATE TOPPING
½ cup raw cashew nuts, soaked in water for 4 hours, drained, and rinsed
2 tablespoons raw cacao powder
2 tablespoons melted cold-pressed extra virgin coconut oil
2 tablespoons melted raw unsweetened creamed coconut
¼ cup raw honey

1. You will need a dehydrator for this recipe. If you don't have a dehydrator, an electric oven may have a setting to dehydrate food on a low enough heat. It may be the defrost setting or slightly higher, or a designated dehydrate setting. Check you have the correct temperature with an oven thermometer before dehydrating in a standard oven.

2. Soak two-thirds of the pumpkin and sunflower seeds in water for 4 hours. Drain and rinse.

3. Line an 8-inch shallow container with nonstick parchment paper. (If using the oven, line an oven pan with parchment paper.) Set aside.

4. Grind the soaked almonds and seeds in a food processor. Add the flaxseed, agave nectar, and cinnamon to the processor and pulse until well combined. Transfer the mixture to a mixing bowl.

5. Add the rest of the seeds to the bowl with the soaked goji berries, cacao nibs, goldenberries, sesame seeds, buckwheat flour, and creamed coconut. Stir well.

6. Press the mixture into the prepared container and dehydrate on high (140°F) for an hour, then on low (115°F) for 3 hours.

7. Remove the mixture from the pan and cut into 10 bars. Line a dehydrator tray with a nonstick dehydrator sheet. (If using the oven, use a parchment-lined oven pan.) Transfer the bars to the sheet and dehydrate again on low until they are dry on the outside but still a little soft on the inside.

8. Meanwhile, make the topping. Pulse the soaked cashew nuts in a clean food processor until smooth and creamy. Spoon into a mixing bowl, add the rest of the ingredients, and mix well with a fork.

9. When the bars are completely cool, coat them with the chocolate topping and chill in the refrigerator until set.

PER BAR: 363 CALS | 25.6G FAT | 8.4G SAT FAT | 30.9G CARBS | 18.3G SUGARS | 7.4G FIBER | 10.1G PROTEIN | TRACE SODIUM

CASHEW COOKIES

These energy-boosting, nut-packed cookies couldn't be any easier to make. Soft-centered and light, but without all the refined sugar, you'll be making them for kids and adults alike.

MAKES: 16 COOKIES
PREP: 10 MINS, PLUS SOAKING AND DEHYDRATING

¾ cup raw cashew nuts, soaked in water
for 4 hours, drained, and rinsed
¾ cup plus 2 tablespoons raw coconut flour,
plus 1 tablespoon for dusting
¼ cup raw coconut milk
2 tablespoons raw agave nectar
½ teaspoon sea salt
½ teaspoon seeds from 1 vanilla bean

1. You will need a dehydrator for this recipe. If you don't have a dehydrator, an electric oven may have a setting to dehydrate food on a low enough heat. It may be the defrost setting or slightly higher, or a designated dehydrate setting. Check you have the correct temperature with an oven thermometer before dehydrating in a standard oven.

2. Pulse the soaked cashew nuts into a food processor until you have a smooth nut butter.

3. Sift the coconut flour into a mixing bowl and stir in the cashew butter along with the remaining ingredients. Mix well with a fork until you have a soft dough.

4. Cover the dough and chill in the refrigerator for 2 hours. Meanwhile, line a dehydrator tray with a nonstick dehydrator sheet and set aside. (If using the oven, line an oven pan with parchment paper.)

5. Roll the chilled dough into 16 small balls, using your hands. Place them on the prepared sheet and flatten a little. (If using the oven, add the balls to your oven pan lined with parchment paper.) Using a fork, make a row of lines over the surface of each cookie. Dust with a sifted tablespoon of coconut flour.

6. Dehydrate the cookies on low (115°F) for about 10 hours, or until they are lightly crisp on the outside but still a little soft in the center. Store in the refrigerator.

FLOUR POWER
Try using almond flour and almond butter
for a different flavor.

PER COOKIE: 68 CALS | 4G FAT | 1.6G SAT FAT | 4.6G CARBS | 2.9G SUGARS | 3.6G FIBER | 2.4G PROTEIN | 80MG SODIUM

NO-BAKE
CARROT CAKE

Tender shavings of carrot are a perfect addition to any cake or dessert,
but they taste particularly sweet and juicy in a raw dessert.

SERVES: 8
PREP: 20 MINS, PLUS SOAKING AND CHILLING

4 carrots, coarsely chopped
²/₃ cup coarsely chopped fresh coconut white meat
²/₃ cup sun-dried organic apricots
³/₄ cup raw walnuts
8 Medjool dates, pitted
½ cup plus 1 tablespoon buckwheat flour
⅓ cup plus 2 tablespoons raw coconut flour
1 teaspoon ground cinnamon
½ teaspoon sea salt
2 tablespoons orange juice
8 raw walnut halves, to decorate

RAW CASHEW CREAM
1½ cups raw cashew nuts, soaked in water for 4 hours,
drained, and rinsed
2 tablespoons orange juice
2½ tablespoons melted cold-pressed
extra virgin coconut oil
2 tablespoons maple syrup

1. Line a 7-inch round cake pan with nonstick parchment paper and set aside.

2. To make the cashew cream, blend the soaked nuts with half the orange juice in a food processor until creamy, then add the remaining ingredients and process until smooth. Transfer the cream to a bowl and keep in the refrigerator

3. For the cake, pulse the carrots and coconut in a food processor for a few seconds, then add the apricots, half the walnuts, and half the dates. Process until everything is finely chopped.

4. Transfer the cake batter to a large mixing bowl. Coarsely chop the remaining walnuts and dates, and add to the bowl. In a separate bowl, combine the flours, cinnamon, and salt, then add to the cake batter and combine thoroughly until all the flour is incorporated. Add the orange juice and stir well.

5. Spoon half the cake batter evenly into the prepared pan. Top with half the cashew cream and smooth the top. Freeze for 2 hours.

6. Remove the cake from the freezer and spoon the rest of the cake batter over the cream. Top with the remaining cream. Freeze for an additional hour, then decorate with the walnut halves.

CREATE, THEN DECORATE
Decorate the finished cake as you want—instead of the walnuts, you could try sun-dried fruit pieces, such as apricots or mangoes.

PER SERVING: 460 CALS | 26.9G FAT | 9.2G SAT FAT | 50.9G CARBS | 31.2G SUGARS | 9.8G FIBER | 10.2G PROTEIN | 160MG SODIUM

ALMOND AND PISTACHIO BROWNIES

These brownies taste incredibly indulgent, but are in fact low in sugar and full of healthy ingredients. As an added bonus, they provide antioxidants, vitamin E, iron, fiber, and monounsaturated fats.

MAKES: 16 BROWNIES
PREP: 10 MINS, PLUS CHILLING

³/₄ cup plus 2 tablespoons raw almonds
³/₄ cup raw pistachio nuts
2 tablespoons raw cacao powder
12 Medjool dates, pitted
1 teaspoon seeds from 1 vanilla bean
1 teaspoon sea salt
¹/₂ cup raw cacao nibs, chopped

TOPPING
3 tablespoons raw cacao powder
³/₄ cup raw honey
2 tablespoons melted cold-pressed extra virgin coconut oil
¹/₂ teaspoon seeds from 1 vanilla bean
¹/₄ cup raw almond milk
1 tablespoon chopped raw pistachio nuts, to decorate

1. Line an 8-inch square baking pan with nonstick parchment paper and set aside.

2. Reserve 3 tablespoons of the almonds and 2¹/₂ tablespoons of the pistachio nuts. Pulse the remaining nuts in a food processor until you have fairly fine crumbs. Add the cacao powder, dates, vanilla seeds ,and salt, and pulse again to form a thick mixture.

3. Transfer the brownie mixture to a bowl and stir in the reserved nuts and the cacao nibs. Press it evenly into the prepared pan.

4. To make the topping, blend the cacao powder, honey, coconut oil, and vanilla seeds in a blender with enough of the almond milk to make a fairly thick sauce. Pour the sauce over the brownie mixture and sprinkle with the pistachio nuts. Chill in the refrigerator for an hour or until the topping is set.

5. Cut the brownie into 16 squares and store in the refrigerator.

SWAP THE NUTS
For another nutty and equally delicious brownie, replace the almonds and pistachio nuts with walnuts and pecans.

PER BROWNIE: 181 CALS | 9.7G FAT | 2.6G SAT FAT | 24.9G CARBS | 17.7G SUGARS | 4.7G FIBER | 4.1G PROTEIN | 160MG SODIUM

PASTEL MELTS

Serve these pretty little treats as part of a buffet or to impress your guests at the end of a dinner party. They come in three different flavors and melt in the mouth.

MAKES: 15 MELTS
PREP: 15 MINS, PLUS CHILLING

LEMON MELTS
$\frac{1}{3}$ cup plus $1\frac{1}{2}$ tablespoons ground almonds
2 tablespoons raw coconut flour
1 tablespoon plus 1 teaspoon lemon juice
$1\frac{1}{2}$ teaspoons raw agave nectar
1 tablespoon melted cold-pressed
extra virgin coconut oil
pinch sea salt
2 tablespoons grated fresh coconut

PISTACHIO MELTS
$\frac{1}{4}$ cup raw pistachio nuts
$2\frac{1}{2}$ tablespoons ground almonds
2 tablespoons raw coconut flour
$1\frac{1}{2}$ teaspoons raw agave nectar
$1\frac{1}{2}$ tablespoons melted cold-pressed
extra virgin coconut oil
$\frac{1}{2}$ teaspoon seeds from 1 vanilla bean
pinch sea salt

MANGO MELTS
$\frac{1}{3}$ cup plus $1\frac{1}{2}$ tablespoons ground almonds
2 tablespoons raw coconut flour,
plus 1 tablespoon for dusting
2 tablespoons pureed fresh mango
$1\frac{1}{2}$ teaspoons raw agave nectar
$1\frac{1}{2}$ teaspoons melted cold-pressed
extra virgin coconut oil
$\frac{1}{2}$ teaspoon seeds from 1 vanilla bean
pinch sea salt

1. To make the lemon melts, combine all the ingredients, except the grated coconut, in a small mixing bowl. Using your hands, form the mixture into five balls and roll them in the coconut. Transfer to a plate and chill in the refrigerator for 30 minutes.

2. To make the pistachio melts, grind the pistachio nuts in a processor. Set aside 2 tablespoons of the ground pistachio nuts and add the rest to a small mixing bowl with the remaining ingredients. Mix thoroughly, then form the mixture into five balls and roll them in the remaining ground pistachio nuts. Transfer to a plate and chill in the refrigerator for 30 minutes.

3. To make the mango melts, combine all the ingredients, except 1 tablespoon of the coconut flour, in a small mixing bowl, then form the mixture into five balls. Sift the remaining coconut flour over them. Transfer to a plate and chill in the refrigerator for 30 minutes.

4. Take the melts out of the refrigerator about 5 minutes before serving.

PAPAYA MELT
You can also make papaya melts by mixing $\frac{1}{3}$ cup plus $1\frac{1}{2}$ tablespoons ground almonds, 2 tablespoons ripe papaya flesh, $1\frac{1}{2}$ teaspoons melted coconut oil, and $\frac{1}{2}$ teaspoon of vanilla bean seeds. Roll the mixture into five balls, decorate with 2 tablespoons of grated fresh coconut, and chill for 30 minutes.

PER LEMON MELT: 95 CALS | 8G FAT | 3.6G SAT FAT | 3.8G CARBS | 2.4G SUGARS | 2.5G FIBER | 2.3G PROTEIN | 120MG SODIUM
PER PISTACHIO MELT: 108 CALS | 9.3G FAT | 4.4G SAT FAT | 4.2G CARBS | 2.4G SUGARS | 2.5G FIBER | 2.6G PROTEIN | 120MG SODIUM
PER MANGO MELT: 82 CALS | 6.1G FAT | 1.9G SAT FAT | 4.3G CARBS | 3G SUGARS | 2.9G FIBER | 2.5G PROTEIN | 120MG SODIUM

INDEX